Fly and the Fly-Bottle

Encounters with British Intellectuals

Fly and the Fly-Bottle

Encounters with British Intellectuals

by
Ved Mehta

COLUMBIA UNIVERSITY PRESS / NEW YORK

1983

The material in this book originated
in *The New Yorker*.
Copyright © 1961, 1962, by Ved Mehta.
Preface to the Morningside Edition © 1983 by Ved Mehta.
Introduction © 1983 by Columbia University Press.

Originally published in book form by Atlantic-Little, Brown.

Illustrations by Steinberg used by permission of the artist.

Library of Congress Cataloging in Publication Data

Mehta, Ved, 1934–
Fly and the fly-bottle.

Reprint. Originally published: Boston: Little,
Brown, 1963. With new introd. and preface.
1. Philosophers—Great Britain. 2. Historians—Great
Britain. 3. Historiography—Great Britain. I. Title.
B1615.M43 1983   192   82-22024
ISBN 0-231-05618-4
ISBN 0-231-05619-2 (pbk.)

Columbia University Press Morningside Edition 1983
Columbia University Press, New York

*Clothbound editions of Columbia University Press books are Smyth-sewn
and printed on permanent and durable acid-free paper.*

For William Shawn

*For one day in thy courts
is better than a thousand.*
—Psalm 84

"What is your aim in philosophy?—To show the fly the way out of the fly-bottle."

LUDWIG WITTGENSTEIN
"Philosophical Investigations"

Contents

Introduction

by Jasper Griffin

It is not often that a book is written on academics and
their altercations which can be found "tremendously
exhilarating" by the (Manchester) *Guardian* and "magnifi-
cently exhilarating" by the New York *Times*. Twenty years
have passed since Ved Mehta put the cat among the professorial pigeons; faced with his inimitable blend of inno-
cence and irony, philosophers and historians revealed their
reasoning and also their rancor, their devotion to truth and
also their all too human attitudes and motives. A. J. Ayer
told him that the *sine qua non* of philosophers was vanity,
and his encounters with historians do not discountenance
the view that they, too, have their full share of it. Some
reviewers were rather shocked by the irreverence they
detected beneath the elegant prose, but then people were
shocked easily in those distant days; this is by no means a
cynical book.

I was one of the people whom Ved Mehta absorbed in his composite "John," the pipe-smoking amateur who helps out with the philosophy. Not all readers have warmed to "John," who is not exempted from the irony of the author. Living in Oxford, surrounded by philosophers, how does a fraction of "John" find that Oxford philosophy looks twenty years after?

The prophecy made in 1962 that the Oxford school would soon break up has come true. At the end of the fifties, one could speak of an orthodoxy: an almost universal belief in ordinary language as the real subject of philosophical inquiry, and as the final court of appeal for all philosophical questions. One consequence of that belief was that many philosophers of the past were "not interesting," because what they said could not be seen as pursuing that sort of inquiry; and many of the traditional questions were "pseudo problems," diseases of language, which cool and scrupulous analysis would eventually cure forever. It was in a whisper that a contemporary put to me in 1959 the subversive suspicion that "behind every pseudo problem there may be a real problem." The history of the subject seemed shorter at that time than ever before or since, consisting only of certain works of Plato and Aristotle, Descartes, Berkeley, Locke, Hume, and Kant, then a horrid gap until the renaissance of true philosophy with Russell and Moore, who gave birth, in turn, to Wittgenstein. G. R. Mure was known as the Last of the Hegelians, as picturesque and irrelevant a creature as the Last of the Mohicans. Many of the names conventionally honored in histories of philosophy evoked from the experts nothing more than a sad smile.

Another consequence was that it seemed harder and harder to make language ordinary enough for truly philosophical discourse. "I'm afraid I don't understand that" was a reply uttered in those days with great self-righteousness, the implication being that what had just been said was deficient in true ordinariness and must be reworded to meet a more exacting standard. It was felt to be a very strong defense, not only intellectually but also morally. ("You are confused or pretentious, or both; my inability to understand is proof of virtue.") Except in the hands of a master like J. L. Austin, that sort of attitude could be pretty deadening. I am struck, also, by the insularity of the scene at that time. The great philosophers lived in Oxford or nearby; most other countries were philosophically dead, and the function even of English-speaking ones was to produce not masters but pilgrims.

That narrowness has, I think, largely passed. On the list of lectures given in philosophy in Oxford this year I see startling names: Duns Scotus, Heidegger, Derrida, even "Topics in Hegel." (The Mohicans are still breeding, after all.) The characteristic juxtaposition of technical and informal language is still to be found: there are lectures on "What You Can Do with Partial-Valued Logic" and on "What a Theory of Meaning Isn't." The star of Wittgenstein has waned a little in England as it has waxed in Germany and Austria; the Austrian village of Trattenbach, where for some years he taught schoolchildren, has laid out a sort of Wittgensteinian Stations of the Cross, with sayings from the Master's works inscribed on the trees to edify the pious tourist. In Oxford, the mathematical logician Frege now interests philosophers at least as much. American names, too — Chomsky, Kripke, Quine, Rawls — could hardly fail to be mentioned in any account of the main controversies in the subject now.

Philosophy has become more technical. Ordinary language gives place to the rigors of generative grammar; new kinds of logic have to be mastered; the philosophy of perception is related more intimately to the study of the physiology of the brain. But this development has been gradual, not abrupt, and most of those who were interviewed for this book are still active in the subject, practicing it in ways not so different from those of twenty years ago.

It might seem that there is a more striking difference: the decline of the really big public row. Even historians, that combative breed, appear to an outsider to go in less nowadays for the full-scale donnybrook, with no holds barred, and opponents comparing each other to Hitler. (See Trevor-Roper on Toynbee.) When we think of quarrelsome historians, we think of the same old stagers whose disobliging comments on their colleagues are one of the pleasures of this book. Specialization has had something to do with it; so, perhaps, has a change in the intellectual atmosphere.

In the thinner, chillier air of the last few years, the universities have been on the defensive. Public money is drying up, and public interest seems to be drying up, too;

the swashbuckler is a rarer type, as that unquestioning belief in the supreme importance of one's work and oneself
which is vital to the aggressive controversialist becomes
harder and harder to retain. Most academics, then, are
keeping their heads down and concentrating on intensive
cultivation of their own plots of scholarly ground.

The theory is neat; it is sad to find that the facts do not
really support it. We have only to turn our attention from
philosophy and history to university Departments of English to find the battle in full swing. There dons of different critical persuasions write brutal reviews of each other's
books and send letters of infuriated protest and denuncia-
tion to the journals in which their own works are brutally
reviewed. The correspondence columns of the *London Review of Books*, fortnight by fortnight, have splendid examples of the Retort Discourteous and the Riposte Re-
sentful. Allegations of prejudice, of charlatanry — even of
malpractice — fly about. The well-publicized rumpus at
Cambridge in 1981 over the refusal of tenure to a lecturer
in English: that would have been a perfect starting point
for another chapter by Ved Mehta. It would be delightful
to have his lucid and rational guidance among the dreaded
bogies of structuralism and hermeneutics and destructur-
alizing, and his deft vignettes of the men and their passions; but that would be another story.

Very soon after King Ptolemy of Egypt set up the first
Western university, at Alexandria, a satirist wrote a poem
comparing the scholars whom the King recruited for his
great Library to exotic birds, "quarrelling in the bird cage
of the Muses." Quarrelsomeness is a characteristic that has

at most periods attached itself to the learned; as peace breaks out on one academic front, the bullets start to fly on another. *Fly and the Fly-Bottle* is a report on a particular place and time, piquantly spiced and individual; it is also a chapter in the more general story of the greatness and littleness of men and women in the unending pursuit of knowledge.

The difficulty in writing about academics is to do justice to both those qualities. The life of study and thought is arduous, demanding not only intellectual powers but also moral qualities: tenacity, sincerity, humility. It is easy to admire the great qualities of eminent scholars and to disregard their weaknesses; it is even easier to ignore their greatness and to gloat over their absurdities. The real challenge is to see both sides: vain, fallible, passionate human creatures, nobly striving to understand and explain the world. Ved Mehta approaches them in the only way that leads to understanding: not without irony, but also not without love.

J. G.

Balliol College, Oxford
November, 1982

Preface to the
Morningside Edition

The idea of writing about Oxford philosophy was first suggested to me by William Shawn, the editor of *The New Yorker*, one day over lunch in 1960. I was immediately taken with it. I had just spent three happy years at the university, and my mind was steeped in the Oxford atmosphere. I was glad of a chance to return to the old place and write about it, with philosophy as the window. Also, for a short time there I had read in the Honours School of P.P.E. (Philosophy, Politics, and Economics) — attending the lectures of several philosophers, among them J. L. Austin, Gilbert Ryle, and Isaiah Berlin, and writing several essays for my philosophy tutor, John Corbett, on problems like "Are There Universals?" The economics part of the P.P.E. syllabus had proved a stumbling block — I had no head for graphs and mathematics — and I had had to abandon P.P.E., but not before I became permanently intoxicated by the fumes of Oxford philosophy. As it happened, the Oxford of my day was the unrivalled seat of philosophical thought, and its philosophy seemed to permeate the stones of every college and the syllabus of every Honours School. I can't account for this preëminence, but I suppose that at certain times in certain places — as at Harvard in Santayana's day or at Cambridge in Bertrand Russell's day — remarkable men and women cluster and flower. They create an ambience. They affect each other's work. Their thought has resonances far beyond the sphere of their discipline or of their activities.

Though I was eager to write about Oxford philosophy, I realized that the project was not without its hazards. Oxford philosophers routinely wrote about each other and each other's work; I would be a layman writing for the general reader. However diligent I was — however deeply I immersed myself in the philosophical literature and in the talk of Oxford philosophers, and tried to convey their interests and preoccupations, the nature and quality of their thinking — I was bound to raise some hackles. Then, too, the philosophers were insiders, who bore family resemblances to one another, as it were, and who relied on their academic credentials to back up their opinions; I would be an outsider — or, at best, an Oxford prodigal son — with no credentials and no opinions to speak of. Besides, I intended to use the reportorial method, which, though it was used as a matter of course with politicians and the like, had never, as far as I knew, been tried on (for want of a better word) intellectuals. Above all, I was aware even from my little exposure that Oxford philosophers were men and women of fine sensibility and delicate, nervous temperament; they tended to have extraordinary intellectual powers and a special cast of mind. These traits made them interested in questions that ordinary people found abstruse or funny. They also had a certain purity of character, and were unusually sensitive to what was said or written about them. And these traits sometimes made them seem to ordinary people fussy and pedantic. By writing about them at all, therefore, I was bound to lay myself open to many charges — that I had abused my Oxford ties, that I was invading people's privacy, that I was vulgarizing a scholarly field. But I decided to brave the treacherous waters and set sail for Oxford philosophy. I had faith in the ability of a layman and an outsider to shed light on areas that often remained hidden from the professionals and insiders themselves, and I thought that my Oxford ties would be a help in getting things right. Nor was I unduly troubled by the privacy issue; many of the philosophers I wished to write about — unlike their nineteenth-century German predecessors, say — were public men and women, who jousted with one another in the press, who lectured all around the world, who debated on television, who often pontificated on subjects beyond the narrow interests of philosophical scholarship. I felt that the Oxford philosophers, far from being the augustly dispassionate scholars of the popular conception, had biases and attitudes every bit as strong as those of politicians. They had personal quirks, and subtle and enduring personal relationships; and these, I believed, affected what they thought and what they wrote. Indeed, in my view, their habits, their dress, their friendships, the remarks they made, what their students thought of them were all, in varying degrees, illuminating. I sometimes even thought — quite unphilosophically — that the positions of Oxford philosophers could be illuminated by recourse to their biographies or to the opinions of them held by other Oxford philosophers.

Writing about Oxford historians and their professional kinsmen, and how they all approached history, was a natural outgrowth of writing about Oxford philosophy. As Thucydides is supposed to have asserted, history is philosophy learned from examples, and it happened that the constellation of historians at Oxford at the time was every bit as luminous as that of the philosophers. Moreover, after abandoning P.P.E. I had read Modern History, and knew the work and the personality of practically every historian there. I braved the treacherous waters a second time, mindful at each compass bearing of the old hazards.

The philosophy chapters of "Fly and the Fly-Bottle" originally appeared as an article in *The New Yorker* in 1961, and the history chapters as a series in 1962. Afterward, I had lengthy letters from most of the people I had written about. Their reactions to my account were as varied as they were themselves. One of them said she was delighted to discover things about herself that she hadn't noticed before. Another, who had apparently never had the experience of seeing his speech directly quoted in print, was indignant that I hadn't paraphrased his comments. A third was gleeful because he felt he finally knew what his colleagues "really" thought. A fourth couldn't believe that he had said what he did say. A fifth was relieved that I had respected his wishes and used him only as a background source. Some accused me of being inaccurate, others of being overaccurate. Many wished to revise or clarify, to amend or elaborate, and since there was a hiatus between the *New Yorker* articles and the publication of the book I was happy to accommodate them whenever I thought they had a point. Some of the letters were elegant essays in themselves, but I cannot reproduce or quote any of them here without sounding either self-congratulatory or self-denigrating; and without violating the sanctity of private communication, not to mention touching off new controversies — those waters remain as treacherous as ever.

The book was published in 1963, by Atlantic–Little, Brown in the United States and by Weidenfeld & Nicolson in the United Kingdom, and in 1965, on both sides of the Atlantic, by Penguin Books in its Pelican series. It has been virtually unavailable in English since 1967. (It continues, apparently, to be available in Japanese and Spanish translations.) But there has been a small but steady demand for it, or so it seems from inquiries I have received over the years from university teachers and librarians. Hence a second edition.

In rereading "Fly and the Fly-Bottle" for this edition — I had not reread it since I corrected the first set of book proofs, some twenty years ago — I was tempted to revise it, or, at least, to update it. I resisted the impulse, though, because I realized that the book, laced as it is with meetings and talks, is a journal of thought at a particular time, and to tamper with it would be like tampering with an old letter. A good part of the book is based on first impressions of people, and first impressions have a particular force; even when, in the course of writing it, I had subsequent meetings with the people in question, I found myself returning to my first impressions as to the relevant point of the compass. And an account of a meeting can never really date: it has a feeling both of freshness and of permanence. The drama of a running explanation and interpretation of one person by another — including the heard speech and intonation, the observed mannerisms, the remembered concerns — belongs to one definite, timeless moment.

In this preface, however, I can suggest what has happened since the early nineteen-sixties to people I discussed or talked to — mostly by setting down one or two public facts of the *Who's Who* variety. Elizabeth Anscombe has continued to translate and edit the posthumous works of Ludwig Wittgenstein; she became a professor of philosophy at the University of Cambridge. A. J. Ayer was knighted, published a memoir, "Part of my Life," and received a *Festschrift*, which includes his replies to his critics; he is a fellow of Wolfson College, Oxford. Sir Isaiah Berlin received the Order of Merit, served as the president of the British Academy, and is bringing out his fugitive essays in four volumes. Ernest Gellner, who became professor of philosophy at the London School of Economics, has published, among other books, "The Devil in Modern Philosophy." Stuart Hampshire was knighted and became the Warden of Wadham College, Oxford. Richard Hare became White's Professor of Moral Philosophy at Oxford. Iris Murdoch was made a Commander of the British Empire and has published a stream of novels and philosophical discourses. Peter Strawson was knighted and became Waynflete Professor of Metaphysical Philosophy at Oxford. G. J. Warnock became the Principal of Hertford College, Oxford. John Brooke has been working on the eighteenth- and nineteenth-century Parliamentary records and is currently editing Horace Walpole's memoirs. E. H. Carr has continued his big work on Russian history. Christopher Hill served as the Master of Balliol College, Oxford, and has published half a dozen more books on the seventeenth century. Iulia (now Julia) Namier has written a life of her husband, entitled "Lewis Namier." A. J. P. Taylor gave up his tutorial fellowship at Magdalen College to pursue his career of journalism, history writing, and broadcasting in London; he has also published an autobiographical essay, "Accident Prone, or What Happened Next." Hugh Trevor-Roper was made a life peer and became the Master of Peterhouse, Cambridge. C. V. Wedgwood became a Dame Commander of the British Empire and received the Order of Merit. Pieter Geyl died in 1966, Earl Russell in 1970, Arnold Toynbee in 1975, Gilbert Ryle in 1976, Sir George Clark and Sir Herbert Butterfield in 1979.

V. M.

New York
November, 1982

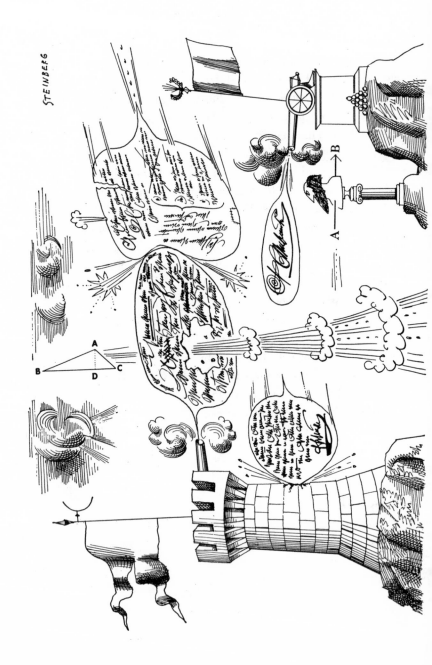

A Battle Against the Bewitchment of Our Intelligence

I'VE spent some happy years in Oxford, and to keep in touch with England I read her newspapers. I am most at home with the *Guardian*, but I also like to look at the correspondence columns of the *Times*, where, in an exception to the *Times* tradition of anonymity, the writers are identified by name and speak directly to the reader. I relish a contest of words, and the *Times* page of letters becomes for me a street where I can stroll each morning and see the people of England — lords and commoners — shake hands, spit at each other, and set off verbal barrages. I began taking this engaging daily walk during my undergraduate years at Balliol College, Oxford, and I've kept up the habit, whether I have found myself in Paris, Damascus, New Delhi, or New York. One autumn day in 1959, as I was taking my intellectual promenade, I met Bertrand Russell, under a signboard reading "Review Refused." "Messrs. Gollancz have recently published a book by Ernest Gellner called 'Words and Things,'" he said as he hailed me. "I read this book before it was published and considered it a careful and accurate analysis of a certain school of philosophy, an opinion which I expressed in a preface. I now learn that Professor Ryle, the editor of *Mind*, has written to Messrs. Gollancz refusing to have this book reviewed in *Mind*, on the ground that it is abusive and cannot therefore be treated as a contribution to an academic subject. Such a partisan view of the duties of an editor is deeply shocking. The merit of a work of philosophy is always a matter of opinion, and I am not surprised that Professor Ryle disagrees with my estimate of the work, but *Mind* has hitherto, ever since its foundation, offered a forum for the discussion of all serious and competent philosophical work. Mr. Gellner's book is not 'abusive' except in the sense of not agreeing with the opinions which he discusses. If all books that do not endorse Professor Ryle's opinions are to be boycotted in the pages of *Mind*, that hitherto respected periodical will sink to the level of the mutual-admiration organ of a coterie. All who care for the repute of British philosophy will regret this."

I did care for the repute of British philosophy. It is, in a sense, a dominant philosophy, with Existentialism, in the present-day world. I had gone up to Oxford with the idea of studying it — British philosophy has its home there and indeed is known generally as "Oxford philosophy," even though its detractors, taking their cue from its so-considered petty linguistic concerns, insist on calling it linguistic philosophy. However, just reading a few essays on philosophical subjects to my tutor made me realize that the linguistic inquiries then being undertaken at Oxford had little connection with what I understood by philosophy, so I immediately abandoned it and took up history instead. Now I recalled that Gellner was a Reader in Sociology at the London School of Economics, a home for angry intellectual orphans, while Gilbert Ryle was Wayneflete Professor of Metaphysical Philosophy at Oxford, from which he edited the extremely influential, eighty-five-year-old philosophical journal *Mind*. The notion of an attack on Oxford thinkers interested me, and I dashed off a letter to Blackwell's, my favorite bookshop, for Gellner's book. While I waited for it to arrive, I impatiently read the subsequent issues of the *Times*, eager to see Earl Russell's gauntlet taken up, preferably by Ryle. It was. This important spokesman of the philosophical Establishment replied four days after Russell's challenge. His communication was terse, to the point, and full of references for diligent readers: "In the book referred to by Earl Russell . . . about 100 imputations of disingenuousness are made against a number of identifiable teachers of philosophy; about half of these occur on pages 159-192 and 237-265."

The shooting had just begun. An eighty-seven-year-old philosopher, out of humor with "a certain school of philosophy," had clashed with its standard-bearer, and neither of them lacked a retinue. The day after Ryle's note appeared, the *Times* carried a third letter under the heading of the week, "Review Refused," this one written by a correspondent named Conrad Dehn. "If the imputations are justified," Dehn argued, "this could not be a good ground [for Ryle's refusal to review Gellner's book], while if they are not I should have thought a review in *Mind* would provide an excellent, even a welcome, opportunity to rebut them." There was also a letter from G. R. G. Mure, the last of the English Hegelians and the Warden of Merton College, Oxford. He, too, was on the side of Russell. "In a tolerably free society," the Warden wrote, "the ban, the boycott, even the too obtrusively cold shoulder, tend to promote the circulation of good books as well as bad. One can scarcely expect that the linguistical Oxford philosophy tutors, long self-immunized to criticism, will now rush to Blackwell's, but I am confident that their pupils will." I was delighted that Mure had taken this occasion to speak out against any philosophical establishment; while I was at the university, the undergraduates used to say of the Warden that he couldn't declare his mind, because half a century ago Russell demolished Hegel and since then no respectable philosopher had dared acknowledge himself a Hegelian openly.

On the following day, I found a letter from Gellner himself. "My book," the polemicist wrote, replying to

Ryle, "does not accuse linguistic philosophers of 'disingenuousness.' . . . This word does not occur in it once, let alone one hundred times. It does attack linguistic doctrines and methods as *inherently* evasive. . . . This claim does not require (though it does not exclude) conscious dishonesty. . . . I am sorry to see Professor Ryle resorting to one further device, the exclusion of criticism as indecorous, and thus evading once again the substantive issue of the merits of linguistic philosophy." Gellner's letter left me baffled. I was still wondering whether Ryle had an excuse for not reviewing the book. My skepticism was not shared by a knighted gentleman, Sir Leslie Farrer, private solicitor to the Queen, who appeared on the same page as Gellner. Sir Leslie defended the author of "Words and Things" with a sharp tongue. "Ridicule," he wrote, "is one of the oldest and not the least effective weapons of philosophic warfare, but yet we find Professor Ryle . . . speaking no doubt '*ex cathedra* on a matter of faith or morals,' propounding the dogma that making fun of members of the Sacred College of Linguistic Philosophers is mortal sin. True, Ryle's first description of Gellner was the word 'abusive' and his second that he 'made imputations of disingenuousness,' but those who read 'Words and Things' (and I trust they will be many) may agree with me that 'made fun of' is a more accurate description."

Sir Leslie was the sixth disputant in the Gellner controversy. In the first week of "Review Refused," the

Times must have received many letters on the subject, but of the six that it selected, five took the Gellner-Russell side. The *Times'* five-to-one support of Gellner indicated a confidence in him that, in my opinion, was not completely justified by his letter. Despite encounters with some worldly philosophers while I was an undergraduate, I did not associate public letter-writing with philosophers; I continued to think of them as Olympian sages. Now this bout in the *Times* shattered my view of their serenity. Instead of age and quiet wisdom, they had youth and energy and anger. I pictured in my mind all the philosophers in England racing to the *Times* office with their dispatches now that Gellner's book had given them an occasion for their precious pronouncements. The day after Sir Leslie's letter, the *Times* correspondence page was silent on philosophy, but the Queen's peace was broken the next day by John Wisdom, a Cambridge professor of philosophy, and "Review Refused," already a heap of pelting words, continued to grow. Wisdom's loyalty to Ryle was unquestioning, and resembled that of a cardinal to the Pope. "I do not know whether it was right to refuse a review to Mr. Gellner's book," he asserted. "I have not read it. Lord Russell's letter . . . carried the suggestion that Professor Ryle refused the book a review because it is opposed to Ryle's philosophy. That suggestion I believe to be false." Such a letter could hardly do much to advance Ryle's cause. But the next day — a Saturday — the Russell-Gellner brigade's secure position in the *Times* column was for the time being shaken by the charge of B. F. McGuinness, a Fellow of Queen's College, Oxford. His philosophical fusillade, though undramatic, was extremely effective. He began impressively, "Newman had to meet the following argument: 'Dr. Newman teaches that truth is no virtue; his denials that he teaches this are not to be credited, since they come from a man who teaches that truth is no virtue.' He described it as an attempt to poison the wells. A subtler form of psychological warfare has been discovered. You belabour your opponents for systematic disregard of truth and consistency, but you add later that there is no question of conscious dishonesty. Thus you can safely call them both knaves and fools. If they expostulate with your account of their views and practices, you reply: 'A typical evasion! . . . They would disown their own doctrines when criticized.' If you are charged with being abusive, your answer is: 'I have accused them of nothing but error!' In his letter . . . Mr. Gellner has even managed to use both kinds of riposte at the same time. The following are some of the phrases in his book that seem to me, in their context, tantamount to accusations of dishonesty: 'camouflage' (p. 163), 'evasion' (p. 164), 'pretence' (p. 169), 'spurious modesty' (p. 170), 'invoking rationalizations according to convenience' (p. 171), '[devices] to cow the neophyte into submission' (p. 186), '[refusal to avow an opinion because it] would ruin one's reputation,' 'insinuation' (p. 188), 'trick' (p. 189)." After this letter, I joined up with the minority — Ryle, Wisdom, and McGuinness.

The following Monday, a letter appeared from Kevin Holland, an undergraduate at Worcester College, Oxford. Holland pealed precedents of "imputations of disingenuousness," and he advanced as many facts in support of Gellner's position as McGuinness had advanced in support of Ryle's. "In the 'Philosophy of Leibniz' (1900), for example," he wrote, "Russell accused Leibniz of a kind of intellectual dishonesty. Forty-six years later, this charge was repeated in 'A History of Western Philosophy,' and Aquinas joined Leibniz in the dock. Ten years ago Professor Ryle published a book in which, 'with deliberate abusiveness,' he characterized a belief held by most ordinary people [that man has a soul in his body] as 'the dogma of the Ghost in the Machine.' In spite of their 'abusiveness,' these three books are regarded by many as philosophic classics." I put down the *Times* reconverted by the undergraduate to the Russell-Gellner position that a philosophical work could call names, heap curses on philosophers, and still deserve to be read. It might even turn out to be a classic. For me the battle was over — and the victory, as I now saw it, went to the majority. As for Ryle's indiscretion — the initial injustice — it was more than corrected by the wide discussion in the newspaper. When the book arrived from Blackwell's, I would read it and make up my own mind about its worth.

After a few days, when I looked at the *Times* again, there was a ponderous epistle, in dignified diction, from a Queen's Counsel, Sir Thomas Creed: "Socrates knew that a true philosophy thrives on blunt criticism and accusations. No one, however inept, who sat at the feet of the robust Oxford philosophers of 40 years ago was ever allowed to forget the scene when Socrates, taunted by an exasperated Thrasymachus with being 'a thorough quibbler,' with 'asking questions merely for the sake of malice,' with 'needing a nurse to stop his drivelling,' implored his accuser to abandon his proposed departure from the discussion so that a problem might be further examined between them. So far from refusing review Socrates forced further discussion on the recalcitrant Thrasymachus. . . . Is Socrates forgotten in modern Oxford? Is Plato's 'Republic' no longer read? Many will hope that a purchase of Mr. Gellner's book will enable undergraduates to ask those awkward questions and make those accusations and insinuations of 'evasion,' 'camouflage,' 'pretence,' 'bamboozling,' 'trick,' which caused Oxford philosophy tutors of an earlier generation such unfeigned delight, a delight only exceeded by the relish with which they exploded the arguments of their accusers."

Next day, J. W. N. Watkins was in the paper. I knew something about him from the gossip of the undergraduates in my day, and pegged him immediately as Gellner's man. I had thought it was about time for someone to play the peacemaker, and Watkins' letter was a white flag: "Let all parties concede that 'Words and Things' is often impolite. But having conceded this, let us remember that etiquette is not the most important thing in philosophy. The best way for linguistic philosophers to repel Mr. Gellner's attack is to overcome their squeamishness about its indecorousness and get down to the rebuttal of its arguments." A few days later, Alec Kassman, editor of the journal published by the august Aristotelian Society, faced up to some questions that had been bothering me. His analysis proceeded in the measured rhetoric of an intellectual editorial: "The essential issue is not whether or not Mr. Gellner's book is meritorious; nor whether or not it is abusive; nor whether or not, if abusive, it is therefore unfit for review: it is a fundamental one of professional ethics and its gravamen is contained in one protasis in Earl Russell's letter: 'If all books that do not endorse Professor Ryle's opinion are to be boycotted in the pages of *Mind*,' etc. The charge, therefore, is one of dishonorable conduct in that Professor Ryle abuses his editorial powers so as to suppress criticism of his own views. Clearly, the allegation in general terms is rhetorical: it is more than sufficient if a single case be substantiated. The reply is a direct traverse — that the review was declined on the ground that the book was found abusive. Earl Russell flatly denies this: 'It is not "abusive" except in the sense of not agreeing with the opinions which he discusses' (. . . Professor Ryle's among others). He offers no opinion on the instances indicated by the editor. The moral case has not progressed beyond this stage save that many . . . evidently wishing to support Earl

Russell, depart from him upon this critical point. They (for example, Sir Thomas Creed . . .) seem mostly to claim that the book may well be abusive and no less fit for review on that account. It is quite possible that the editor's claim that an abusive book does not deserve a review in *Mind* is ill-founded or injudicious. That, however, is a side issue, if in fact the view is one which he genuinely held and acted on. The accusation is not that he is unduly sensitive, or unwise, but that he is biased against any critic as such, to the consequent detriment of his journal. . . . He publicly rebutted the specific charge in some detail, and Earl Russell has not replied. It is about time that he did; the pages of *Mind* are available to illustrate editorial policy. The allegation is a disagreeable one, and as serious as could be made against a philosopher in Professor Ryle's position. If Earl Russell can sustain it, he should show this. If he cannot, he should say so, that the reputation of both editor and journal may be cleared. That is the heart of the matter."

Even though Mr. Kassman argued from a position opposed to mine — I was still sticking to the side of Russell-Gellner — I had to admit that he had succeeded in making the best possible defense for Ryle. I made up my mind not to look at any more letters from the philosophical combatants, but I could not help glancing at the succeeding issues of the *Times* just in case Russell should answer Mr. Kassman. Nineteen days after Russell had attacked the philosophical Establishment, he was back in print with a reply. "There are two different points at issue," Russell remarked, closing the controversy. "First, is anything in Mr. Gellner's book 'abusive'? Secondly, should a book containing anything abusive be, on that account alone, refused a review in *Mind*? As to the first point, 'abusive' is not a very precise word. . . . I cannot . . . 'reply' . . . since Professor Ryle has not given a single instance of a single sentence which he considers abusive. It is up to Professor Ryle to quote at least one passage which he considers abusive. This, so far as I know, he has not yet done. As to the second and much more important point, I do not think that a serious piece of philosophical work should be refused a review even if it does contain passages which everybody would admit to be abusive. Take, for example, Nietzsche's 'Beyond Good and Evil.' In this book he speaks of 'that blockhead John Stuart Mill,' and after saying 'I abhor the man's vulgarity,' attributes to him the invention of the Golden Rule, saying: 'Such principles would fain establish the whole of human traffic upon mutual services, so that every action would appear to be a cash payment for something done to us. The hypothesis here is ignoble to the last degree.' I do not accept these opinions of Nietzsche's, but I think a philosophical editor would have been misguided if, on account of them, he had refused a review to 'Beyond Good and Evil,' since this was undoubtedly a serious piece of philosophical work. I note that neither Professor Ryle nor anyone else has denied that the same is true of

Mr. Gellner's book." Firmly turning his back on the philosophical Establishment, Russell stumped resolutely away, carrying most of the medals.

Through the fight over "Words and Things," I acquired a renewed and rather persistent interest in Oxford philosophy. Several English publications ran editorials about the conclusion of hostilities, and I read them eagerly, but they did not tell me very much about the philosophers working in England. The *Times* wrote its typical on-the-one-hand, on-the-other-hand leader. It said, on the one hand, that Gellner's book "caricatures its prey," and that his "barbs are not of the carefully polished kind." It said, on the other hand, that the caricatured philosophers "stick closely to their lasts" with "enviable academic patronage," and regard "philosophical problems as a sort of cerebral neurosis which it is their job to alleviate." The leader in the *Economist* was no more enlightening about the nature of this cerebral neurosis. "Why are modern philosophers hated — if they are?" it asked. "Hardly any of them, despite their other diversity, would claim that, as philosophers, they can tell us what to do. When other direction posts are falling down, philosophers are assumed to be the people who ought to be giving us directions about life. But if they cannot, they cannot." The tone of these two comments was fairly representative of the editorial voice of Britain's intellectual press.

Gellner's book, when it finally arrived, was equally unsatisfactory. It was passionate, polemical, and disjointed, and grouped disparate thinkers indiscriminately — this much was apparent even to a novice like me. The editorials had bewildered me by their opaqueness; Gellner bewildered me by his flood of glaring light, which prevented me from seeing through to the philosophers. At the time of the turbulent correspondence, I was living in America, but I decided that on my next visit to England I would seek out some of the philosophers and talk to them about their activities.

Sometime later, I found myself in London. I wrote to three or four philosophers for appointments and started my researches into contemporary philosophy by approaching an old Oxford friend of mine, even though he is by no means the most unprejudiced person about. As an undergraduate, he read Classics and Greats, the English-speaking world's most thorough study of classical literature, language, history, and philosophy, and — Greats' concession to our age — modern philosophy. All the time he was working at philosophy, he hated it, but he did it as a job, and because he was naturally brilliant, after his Schools (the final degree examination) he was courted to be a professional philosopher at Oxford; he remained true to his temperament, however, and turned down the offer, deciding to sit it out in London until he spotted a good opening in Oxford classics. In the meantime, he has amused himself by composing Greek and Latin verses and prose, and turning the poetry of Hopkins, Pound, Eliot, and Auden into lyrics in the style of the Greek Anthology or of Vergil, Horace, or Petronius. Having been trained in Latin and Greek since the age of six, he reads the literature of these languages almost faster than that of his own country. This classical, or language, education is characteristic of almost all the contemporary English philosophers. Aside from his Victorian training, the most typically philosophical thing about my friend is that he constantly smokes a pipe — a habit that has long been the *sine qua non* of English philosophers. Over some mulled claret late one evening in his Chelsea back-street basement flat, he surveyed the subject of philosophy from the tremulous heights where it had led him, and he talked to me about it too frankly and unprofessionally to wish to be identified, so I'll call him John.

During their four years as undergraduates, the Greats men sit for altogether twenty-four three-hour papers, and John said he imagined that one-third of his time had been spent doing philosophy and preparing for examinations in logic and moral and classical philosophy. "The examination in classical philosophy was straightforward, since it meant, for the most part, reading the works of Plato and Aristotle," he explained. "For logic and moral philosophy we were supposed to do a certain amount of philosophical history, but in fact we did extremely little; we started by doing a tutorial on Descartes and followed it up by writing essays on Locke and Berkeley, and I believe we were meant to do a couple on Hume. But these historical people are just for exercise; they need not be brought into the exam. I never once mentioned them, and the examiners are really rather bored to have you do so, I think." John said that Greats men mostly read contemporary philosophers, because the philosophers at Oxford are concerned only with their own puzzles. They are not very much occupied with problems that interested earlier philosophers, even as little as forty years ago. John actually went into philosophical training when, after dabbling a little in the history of different schools, he read Ludwig Wittgenstein's "Philosophical Investigations" and two books of A. J. Ayer's — "Language, Truth and Logic" and "The Problem of Knowledge," both of which he had to work through several times, once making notes all the way. He was then turned loose on P. F. Strawson's "Introduction to Logical Theory" and "Individuals: An Essay in Descriptive Metaphysics." He read only the first half of "Individuals" and then skimmed the rest, because he couldn't make much sense of it. After Strawson, to John's great relief, came easier volumes, on ethics, by Richard Hare and P. H. Nowell-Smith. But the bulk, and the most important part, of his study was articles in issues of *Mind* and the *Proceedings of the Aristotelian Society* — the richest repositories of Oxford philosophy.

Since the main purpose of the Greats course is not to produce Professor I. Q. but to develop minds, John insisted that his handling of the Schools questions was more important than the list of books and articles he had read. Alas, once the results were published, as custom enjoined, all the Schools papers were burned, and John could reconstruct his brilliant answers only from memory. He considered his logic paper to be the paradigm, both because logic is the centerpiece of Oxford philosophy and because the principles of logic can be applied to other branches of the subject. Examiners therefore tend to read the logic paper with more care than any other. "Um," he began, recalling his paradigm, "there was a question I didn't do: 'Is my hearing a noise in my head as mechanical as the passing of a noise through a telephone?' The suggestion here is: Can our senses be explained away in mechanical terms? One that I did attempt but abandoned was 'Who is Socrates?' — the figure that people greeted when they saw it coming with the words 'Hello, Socrates,' or the person who was Socrates? You clearly can't answer, 'This is the body that went around with Socrates.' It's also not very nice to say, 'This is the body that went around *as* Socrates,' because it sounds as if it went around disguised as Socrates. Since I couldn't make up my mind about this, I couldn't write about it. But a stock old war horse of a question that I did complete was 'If I know that Y is the case, is it possible for me not to know that I know it?' And what I said about it must have been on these lines: To know that a thing is the case is not — this is very straightforward stuff — to have my mind in a certain position. If I know, for instance, that ice melts when the sun shines, this means that when the sun shines I don't go skating. In that case, it's perfectly possible that I don't consciously know that ice melts when the sun shines. But the question now arises of whether I know it unconsciously, and the answer is that it's possible never to have considered this. But to analyze it still further: Once you do ask yourself whether you know it unconsciously, can you give yourself the wrong answer? And I think the answer to this is — Now, I wonder what I said. Um. Well. Yes. The answer is that you sometimes say, 'I don't know whether I know it unconsciously; I don't know whether I really know it or whether I'm just guessing.' So far so good. But can you now go on to say, 'I thought I didn't know that ice melts when the sun shines, but then later on I found out I did'? My conclusion was that you could feel certain you didn't know it, and then when you *came* to it you found out you did. Take this example: Suppose they said 'Do you know how to tie such and such a knot?' and you said 'No.' And then when you were drowning they threw you a line and said 'Tie that knot on your life belt,' and you succeeded in tying it. When you were saved, they would say, 'Well, you did know how to tie it after all, didn't you?' And you could say either 'Yes, I did know all the time, but I was certain that I didn't before I started drowning' or 'I just found out how to do it — it *came* to me when you threw me the line.' "

By now, John was so lost in philosophy that I couldn't have stopped him if I had wished to. He was puffing away madly at his pipe, and, without pausing, he went on to the next question on his logic paper. "My favorite in the paper, however, was the answer to another question: 'Could there be nothing between two stars?' All these Schools questions look very simple till you start thinking about them. What I said about this one was 'There are two senses in which there can be nothing between two stars'— which is always a good way of going at such questions. On the one hand, if there is strictly not anything between two things, then they are together, and if two stars are adjacent, then, clearly, they aren't exactly two stars — they're perhaps a twin star. On the other hand — and this was my second point — if I were to say to you, 'There's absolutely nothing between Oxford and Birmingham,' meaning 'There aren't any restaurants on the road,' or something of that sort, in this sense there isn't anything between two stars. A distinction thus emerges between nothing and *a* nothing, because when you answer the question 'What is there between two stars?' by saying 'There isn't anything between them,' you tend to think there is a nothing, a great lump of nothing, and there it is, holding the stars apart. This, actually, when you think about it, is nonsense, because you can't have 'a nothing,' which naturally led me to discuss the difference between space and *a* space. If you can't say that there's nothing between two stars, neither can you give much account of what there is between them. You tend to say there's a great expanse of Space, with a capital 'S,' and this is not very satisfactory, because the way you use the ordinary word 'space' is to say there is *a* space between my table and my door, and that means you can measure it, and presumably there is a distance between table and door that can be measured. Whereas if you say there is a great lump of Space, that's like saying a great lump of nothing or of time, which, of course, is misleading. My conclusion was that in the loose sense, in which there is nothing between Oxford and Birmingham, there could be nothing between two stars; that is, nothing you could give a name to, or nothing you thought it worth giving a name to, or nothing of the sort that interests you. But in the strict sense there can't be nothing between two stars, because if there were nothing between two stars, the stars would be on top of each other. How tedious, I agree, but I was just giving you this as an example of what Greats people actually do."

We poured some claret, and drank a toast to John's success with Schools and, upon his insistence, to his wisdom in putting the whole subject behind him. He reluctantly drank also to my researches into Oxford philosophy. From his paradigm answer I had received the distinct impression that Oxford philosophy was simplified, if accurate, mental gymnastics, or, at best, intellectual pyrotechnics. But I wasn't sure I had grasped the essence, so I pressed him for his own view, and for a definition. He twitched nervously, offered me some more claret, went into a sort of trance, and said puzzling things like "Philosophy at Oxford is not one thing but many things" and "Some of the philosophers there are in one sense doing the same thing and yet in another sense doing quite different things." And how the things they did were the same and yet different could emerge only by talking about the philosophers individually, and even then I was likely to get them confused. And although he didn't say it, he implied that the best thing for me to do would be to read Greats (of which, of course, modern philosophy is just a part) and, if possible, get acquainted with the philosophers themselves, as "people." He suggested meeting Gellner, as the man who had roughly broken the calm of Oxford philosophy; Russell, as a born controversialist who had served the mistresses of both science and art as no one else had in the twentieth century; Strawson, as an antidote to Russell ("Strawson is now far and away the most original thinker of what is often called the Oxford philosophy"); Ayer, as a brilliant thinker who had his pipeline from Central Europe and whom neither the Russells nor the Strawsons could overlook; Stuart Hampshire, as a philosopher with a civilized view of the whole subject — he had one foot in Continental thought, and the other in the whole history of philosophy; and Richard Hare, who represented the impact of Oxford philosophy on morals — the rights and wrongs of living; and certainly one feminine philosopher, because women's invasion of the field was a sort of twentieth-century philosophical event. Then John went on to use what appeared to me English adaptations of Chinese proverbs, like "We are all squirrels in cages and we go round and round until we are shown the way out." And how was I to find my way out? We were back to reading Greats. To such direct questions as "Is Oxford philosophy, like geometry, suspended in a vacuum?" I received negative answers. "No," he said once, "in one sense we have as much real substance as Socrates, Plato, and Aristotle, and are even doing their sorts of things. But in another sense . . ." I wanted to find my way back to the clarity and confidence of his Schools answers, so I pried at his mind with ancient philosophers (who taught men, among other things, what to do and how to live) for my lenses. "Does each of the Oxford philosophers fancy himself a Socrates?" I asked. "I have never seen them hanging around street corners and athletic rooms, as Socrates did in Athens, with unwashed aristocratic young men, to cheer philosophical disputations and to jeer crowds of fools."

"You're mixed up in a difficult business," he said, pouring me some claret. He went on to explain the connection between the ancients and the contemporaries. "The idea of Greats philosophy," he said, "is that after a few years of work — training in clear and precise thinking — the high-powered undergraduate can unravel any sort of puzzle more or less better than the next man. It makes a technique of being non-technical." He smiled. "Like Socrates, we assume the pose of knowing nothing except, of course, how to think, and that is the only respect in which we consider ourselves superior to other people. For us — as, to a certain degree, it was for him — philosophy is ordinary language (but don't press me about this 'ordinary language'), and so, we choose to think, it ought not to be a technical business. Although he did not know it, Socrates, like us, was really trying to solve linguistic puzzles, and this is especially true in the longer dialogues of Plato — the 'Republic' and the 'Laws'— where we learn quite a lot about Socrates' method and philosophy, filtered, of course, through his devoted pupil's mind. Some of the Pre-Socratics, who provided Plato and his master with many of their problems, were in difficulties about how one thing could be two things at once — say, a white horse. How could you say 'This is a horse and this is white' without saying 'This one thing is two things'? Socrates and Plato together solved this puzzle by saying that what was meant by saying 'The horse is white' was that the horse partook of the eternal, and perfect, Form horseness, which was invisible but really more horselike than any worldly Dobbin; and ditto about the Form whiteness: it was whiter than any earthly white. The theory of Form covered our whole world of ships and shoes and humpty-dumptys, which, taken all in all, were shadows — approximations of those invisible, perfect Forms. Using the sharp tools in our new linguistic chest, we can whittle Plato down to size and say that he invented his metaphysical world of Forms to solve the problem of different kinds of 'is'es; you see how an Oxford counterpart of Plato uses a simple grammatical tool in solving problems like this. Instead of conjuring up an imaginary edifice of Forms, he simply says there are two different types of 'is'es — one of predication and one of identity. The first asserts a quality: 'This is white.' The second points to the object named: 'This is a horse.' By this simple grammatical analysis we clear away the rubble of what were Plato's Forms. Actually, an Oxford philosopher is closer to Aristotle, who often, when defining a thing — for example, 'virtue' — asked himself, 'Does the definition square with the ordinary views of men?' But while the contemporary philosophers do have antecedents, they are innovators in concentrating most of their attention on language. They have no patience with past philosophers: Why bother listening to men whose problems arose from bad grammar? At present, we are mostly preoccupied with language and grammar. No one at Oxford would dream of telling undergraduates what they ought to do, the kind of life they ought to lead." That was no longer an aim of philosophy, he explained, but even though philosophy had changed in its aims and methods, people had not, and that was the reason for the complaining undergraduates, for the bitter attacks of *Times'* correspondents, and even, perhaps, for his turning his back on philosophy.

Both of us more or less stopped thinking at the same time, very much as one puts down an intellectual work when thinking suddenly becomes impossible. "How about some claret?" both of us said. The decanter was empty. We vigorously stirred some more claret, sugar, and spices in a caldron and put the brew on the gas ring, and while we were waiting for a drink, we listened to a portion of "The Magic Flute." I felt very much like Tamino at the Temple of Wisdom, except that my resolution was sinking. The claret revived it, and, with curtains drawn against the night, I pressed on with my researches.

Talking with John, I came to feel that present-day Oxford philosophy is a revolutionary movement — at least when it is seen through the eyes of past philosophers. I asked him about the fathers of the revolution. Again he was evasive. Strictly speaking, it was fatherless, except that Bertrand Russell, G. E. Moore, and Ludwig Wittgenstein — all of them, as it happened, Cambridge University figures — "were responsible for the present state of things at Oxford." Blowing pipe smoke in my direction, John continued, "I think the aspect of Russell's philosophy that will be remembered is his logical atomism, which was proclaimed to the world in a series of lectures in 1918; the driving force of these lectures was a distrust of ordinary speech. He argued at that time that you had to get away from ordinary language (and disastrous grammatical errors of past philosophers — 'is'es again), which did nothing but foster misleading notions, and construct a language on a mechanical model — like the symbolic logic of his and Alfred North Whitehead's 'Principia Mathematica,' published in 1910 — that would in turn correspond to the logical structure of the universe. He thought that you could take any statement and break it up into its atomic parts, for each part would have a meaning, or a reference, or both. What he was trying to do was to build a formal logical system, so that you could do arguments and logic on computers. But it is now thought that, among other things, he confused meaning and reference, and also broke up sentences in a totally wrong way, and therefore his philosophy is considered to be mainly of historical interest."

By now, I felt very much as though I were inside a Temple of Knowledge, if not of Wisdom, and I asked John if he would like to tell me a little bit about Moore, too. He said he wouldn't like to but he would do it, because he supposed he had to. "Moore was a common-sense philosopher," he began. "Almost unphilosophically so. His most famous article was 'A Defense of Common Sense,' which was mostly concerned with morality. His common-sense view was, on the surface, very much like Dr. Johnson's: I am certain that my hand is here because I can look at it, touch it, bang it against the table. While he did distinguish between a naturalistic statement ('The grass is green') and a non-naturalistic statement ('God is good'), he held that we *know* both kinds of statements to be true by intuition. (Goodness was not naturalistic, like green, because it could neither be analyzed in terms of any basic qualities, like greenness or hardness, nor was it itself a basic quality.) On the question 'How do I know the grass is green or God is good?,' he agreed with most people, who would reply,

'Because I know it's so, and if you don't know it's so, too bad!' "

John said that Oxford people owed their faith in ordinary language and ordinary men to Moore. But it was Wittgenstein who made John puff furiously at his pipe. "There are two Wittgensteins, not one," he said. "There is the Wittgenstein of 'Tractatus Logico-Philosophicus,' published in 1921, and the totally different Wittgenstein of 'Philosophical Investigations,' printed posthumously, a quarter of a century later. I'm almost certain to give a misinterpretation of Wittgenstein," John went on humbly but vigorously, "but in the 'Tractatus' he was trying to find out the basic constituents of the world, and in a way his 'Tractatus' attempt was reminiscent of Russell's 1918 try. According to the first Wittgenstein, the world was ultimately made up of basic facts, and these were mirrored in language: accordingly, a proposition was a picture of the world. Now, basic facts were made up of basic objects and basic qualities. The basic objects were sense data — for example, a patch before my eyes, or a feeling in my leg. But these could not exist without having some definite quality. I mean, you could not just have a patch before your eyes — it had to be some definite color. And you could not just have a feeling in your leg — it had to be some definite sort of feeling. When you attached a particular color to the patch or specified the sort of feeling in your leg, you had basic facts, which language mirrored or could mirror. An example of a basic sentence that mirrored a basic fact was 'Here, now, green,' meaning that you had in front of your eyes a sense datum that was green. Just as the world was essentially built out of these basic facts, so language was essentially built out of basic-fact sentences. The business of the philosopher was to break down the complex statements used in language — like 'My wife sees a green table'— into its constituent parts. In the 'Investigations,' Wittgenstein completely gave up his 'Tractatus' ideas, and thought that philosophical perplexity arose because people abused the ordinary ways of speech and used a rule that was perfectly all right in its own area to cover another area, and so they got into a muddle; he thought that you could disentangle the puzzle by pointing out that they were misusing ordinary language. As he wrote, 'Philosophy is a battle against the bewitchment of our intelligence by means of language.' It was like showing, in his most quoted phrase, 'the fly the way out of the fly-bottle.' If in the 'Tractatus' Wittgenstein was like Russell, in 'Philosophical Investigations' he was like Moore, a common-sense man. Wittgenstein now thought that you couldn't ask what the structure of reality was; you could only analyze the language in which people talked about it. A lot of different types of structure were found in language, and it was impossible to assimilate them all under any one heading. He regarded the various ways of expression as so many different pieces in a game of chess, to be manipulated according to certain rules. It was quite wrong to apply the rules of one set of statements to another, and he distinguished several types of statements — for example, common-sense statements about physical objects, statements about one's own thoughts and intentions, and moral propositions. It was the philosopher's job to find out the rules of the language game. Suppose you had been brought up from a small child to play football. By the time you were sixteen, you played it quite according to the rules. You probably didn't know the names of the various rules or what, exactly, they said, but you never made a mistake about them, and when anyone asked you 'Why do you play this way, and not that?' you just said 'Well, I always have played this way.' Now, it would be possible for someone else to come along as an observer and write down what rules you were playing by, if he observed you long enough. Like the observer on the football ground, a philosopher should primarily investigate what the rules used for communication are."

Just when I thought I had absorbed all this, John said, "I hope I haven't left you with the impression that there is necessarily a firm connection between Russell, Moore, and Wittgenstein, on the one hand, and present-day Oxford philosophy, on the other. Some people would argue that the late J. L. Austin, in the fifties White's Professor of Moral Philosophy at Oxford, had as much to do with shaping thinking at the university as anyone else, including Wittgenstein. Also, you mustn't overlook the role of logical positivism in all this." John said he would prefer not to say anything about Austin, because he had very mixed feelings about him. But logical positivism — well, that was another matter. A. J. Ayer, recently appointed Wykeham Professor of Logic at Oxford, was the first Englishman to proclaim the principles of logical positivism to the English intellectual world. After his graduation from Oxford, in 1932, he went to Vienna and made the acquaintance of some of the most famous European philosophers — members of the so-called Vienna Circle — who had come together to discuss, among other things, Wittgenstein's "Tractatus." Ayer made his reputation for life by returning to England six months later and writing "Language, Truth and Logic," a tract of logical positivism. "If I may put it so," John concluded, with a smile, "he has pattered all around the kennel, but he's always been on his Viennese leash."

I knew it was getting late, but I asked John for a little more philosophy, for the road. We had some more claret, and before we packed up for the night, he quickly served up logical positivism.

The logical positivism of the thirties, I learned, was a skeptical movement. It claimed that any statement that could not be *verified* by sense experience was meaningless. Thus, all statements about God, all statements about morality, all value judgments in art were logically absurd. For example, "Murder is wrong" could only mean, at best, "I disapprove of murder," or, still more precisely, "Murder! Ugh!" What made a statement like

"There is a dog in my neighbor's garden" meaningful was that I could *verify* it. If I went into the garden, I could see the dog, beat it with a stick, get bitten, hear it bark, and watch it chew on an old bone.

The room was thick with smoke by now, for John, in a very un-English way, had kept all the windows closed. Both of us were tired. He put on some coffee, and we chatted about this and that, after which, instead of trundling to my own lodgings, I dossed down on his sofa.

The next day, I hung around John's room, trying to sort out my thoughts after the injections of Oxford philosophy administered by the sharp mind of my friend, until the time came for me to call on Gellner, the first philosopher on my list. During the *Times'* siege of Ryle, I had been first pro-Gellner, then anti, then pro, but John had watched the whole affair with the detachment of a philosopher. He gave me a rationalizing explanation: Good editors were eccentric people, and potentates who ruled scholarly periodicals tended to be even more eccentric than their counterparts on popular magazines. Then he handed me a copy of G. E. Moore's autobiography opened to a passage about Moore's editorship of *Mind*, which made me shift my weight about uncomfortably on the Gellner-Ryle seesaw. "In 1920, on Stout's retirement from the Editorship of *Mind*, an office which he had held since the beginning of the 'New Series' in 1892," I read, "I was asked to succeed

him as Editor; I . . . have now been Editor for more
than twenty years. . . . I think . . . that I have succeeded in being impartial as between different schools
of philosophy. I have tried, in accordance with the
principles laid down when *Mind* was started and repeated by Stout in the Editorial which he wrote at the
beginning of the New Series, to let merit, or, in other
words, the ability which a writer displays, and not the
opinions which he holds, be the sole criterion of whether
his work should be accepted. . . . The most noticeable
difference between *Mind* under me and *Mind* under
Stout seems to me to be that under me the number of
book reviews has considerably diminished. This has
been partly deliberate: under Stout there were a great
number of very short reviews, and I have thought
(perhaps wrongly) that very short reviews were hardly
of any use. But it is partly, I am afraid, owing to lack
of thoroughly businesslike habits on my part, and partly
also because, knowing what a tax I should have felt it
myself to have to write a review, I have been shy about
asking others to undertake the task. Whatever the
reason, I am afraid it is the case that I have failed
to get reviewed a good many books which ought to
have been reviewed."

After reading these honest words of Professor Moore
— a good editor and a perfect gentleman, who was
fanatical about avoiding prejudices — I went to see Gellner with an open mind. I got on a bus that would take
me to his home, in S.W. 15, and an hour later I found

myself on the edge of a middle-middle-class settlement where houses stood out sparsely, like so many road signs. Trucks and broken-down little cars sluggishly wheeled themselves through the growing suburbia carrying vegetables, meat, and a few people to the city. A man was standing in front of Gellner's house, holding a baby in his arms. It was Gellner. "Come in! Come in!" he said. Gellner (a man of thirty-four) proved to be dark, of medium height, and casually dressed. His hair was uncombed, and he had the air of an offbeat intellectual. We went inside, and he introduced me to his wife. He was reluctant to talk philosophy while his wife and the infant were in the room, so we chatted about this and that, and I learned that he was born in Paris of Czech parentage, spent his boyhood in Prague, and had come to England with his family just before the war.

When Mrs. Gellner took the baby upstairs, he diffidently pointed out twin tape recorders in a corner of the living room. "These Grundig machines produced 'Words and Things,'" he said. "The Memorette recorded my words and a secretary at the London School of Economics, thanks to this magical Stenorette, transformed my voice into typed copy." He spoke in a quick and rather harassed way, as though the tape recorders were at that moment catching his words on an ever-shrinking spool.

"I was going through the *Times* correspondence the other day," he went on. "I have kept a complete file of it. I was elated to find that most of the people lined up on my side."

As far as Gellner was concerned, I gathered, all philosophers at Oxford were more or less alike, since all of them were interested only in linguistic analysis. ("Oxford philosophy," he said, was a misnomer, since it grouped the philosophers by the setting of their practice, rather than by the linguistic method which they all shared in common.) Instead of regarding philosophy as an investigation of the universe — or knowledge as a sort of inventory of the universe ("There are more things in heaven and earth, Horatio, than are dreamt of in your philosophy"), to which wise men from the beginning of time had been adding — the linguistic philosophers handed over the universe to the students of the natural sciences and limited philosophy to an inquiry into rules of language, the gateway to human knowledge. They analyzed language to determine what could and could not be said and therefore in a sense what could and could not exist. Any employment of words that did not conform to the rules of dictionary usage was automatically dismissed as nonsense. "But I answer," Gellner said, "all words cannot be treated as proper nouns." To clarify his point, he read a passage from one of his Third Programme broadcasts: "The . . . reason why the dictionary does not have scriptural status [according to him, all linguistic philosophers use the Oxford English Dictionary as the Holy Writ of philosophy] is that most expressions are not [proper] names; their meaning is not really exhausted by the specification of their use and the paradigmatic uses that occur in the dictionary. Their meaning is usually connected in a complicated way with a whole system of concepts or words or ways of thinking: and it makes perfectly good sense to say that a word, unlike a name, is mistakenly used in its paradigmatic use. It makes sense to say this *although* we have not done any rechristening and are still continuing to use it in its old sense." He pegged the rest of his criticism on the practitioners of linguistic philosophy.

"Out of the bunch of Oxford philosophers," he said, "I suppose I have the strongest aversion to Austin, who in some ways typified the things I dislike about them most. I found his lecture technique a creeping barrage, going into endless detail in a very slow and fumbling way. He used this style to browbeat people into acceptance; it was a kind of brainwashing. The nearest I got to him was on some committees that we were both members of. I always took some trouble not to get to know him personally, because I disliked his philosophy and I knew that sooner or later I would attack him and I didn't wish to be taken as a personal enemy. With Austin, I had an impression of someone *very* strongly obsessed with never being wrong, and using all kinds of dialectical devices to avoid being wrong. He intimidated me with his immense caginess; like Wittgenstein, he never stated the doctrines he was trying to get across — or, actually, the crucial thing was stated in informal sayings, which never got into print. Thus he artfully shielded himself from challengers. To Oxford philosophers Wittgenstein, like Austin, is another little god who can do no wrong. They like Wittgenstein mainly because he gave up his achievements in the technical field and his power as a mathematical magician for the ordinary language of a plain man — or, rather, the kind of ordinary language that an undergraduate who has studied the classics in Greats can take to pieces."

Linguistic philosophers were thought to alleviate cerebral neurosis, Gellner said. To understand them, he believed, one had to turn to sociology, his present professional interest. "About the social milieu from which these Oxford philosophers arose," he went on rapidly, "I can say nothing except what I have already said in the ninth chapter of my book. On second thought, perhaps there is one improvement that, on the basis of my reading of C. P. Snow, I could have made in my chapter." Gellner said that had Snow's brilliant pamphlet "The Two Cultures and the Scientific Revolution" existed when Gellner wrote his book, he would have invoked it, for Snow's characterization of the two cultures was right up his philosophical alley. "The milieu of linguistic philosophers is a curious one," Gellner continued. "As Sir Charles, in his pamphlet, points out, there are these two cultures — a literary one and a scientific one — and traditionally the literary one has always enjoyed more prestige. But for some time it has been losing ground; technology and science have been taking its place. Only in Oxford has the literary culture managed to retain an unchallenged supremacy. There Greats still remains at the apex of the disciplines, and within Greats the brightest young men are often selected to become philosophers. But is there any intellectual justification for this self-appointed aristocracy? Is there any widespread theory that anybody can subscribe to as to why the Greats form of philosophy is the highest sort of activity? I say no. The literary culture would have perished a long time ago if it weren't for the social snobbery of Oxford and her self-perpetuating philosophers. Linguistic philosophy is nothing more than a defense mechanism of gentleman intellectuals, which they use in order to conceal the fact that they have nothing left to do."

Turning to his Stenorette tape recorder, Gellner asked me, "Would you like to hear something I was dictating this morning? It really sums up my position, and in a sense you could say it is the essence of 'Words and Things.'" I nodded, and he flicked a switch. "Philosophers in the past were proud of changing the world and providing a guide for political life," the voice whispered through the little speaker of the tape recorder. "About the turn of the century, Oxford was a nursery for running an empire; now it is a nursery for leaving the world exactly as it is. The linguistic philosophers have their job cut out for them — to rationalize the loss of English power. This is the sociological background which is absolutely crucial to the understanding of linguistic philosophers."

Gellner stopped the machine and said, "There you have my whole sociological analysis. Full stop. In 'Words and Things,' I used Thorstein Veblen for the sociology of the philosophers. If I were writing the book now, I would use Veblen and Sir Charles."

Gellner picked up a copy of *Commentary* from the coffee table and read me a sentence or two from its review of his book, which implied that he had written "Words and Things" because he had failed to get a cushy job at Oxford. "Dash it, job-hungry people do not write my sort of book," he said. "How nasty can you really get? As far as professional philosophy is concerned, 'Words and Things' ruined my future rather than secured it. I attacked the philosophical Establishment, and as long as the present philosophers remain in power, I will never have a position at an Oxford college. Whether I will be accepted again in philosophical circles remains to be seen."

Gellner offered to drive me back to the city. For transportation he had a small truck, which he used for getting to the London School of Economics when he missed his commuter train. We bounced noisily along the road, Gellner making himself heard intermittently over the engine clatter. He had more or less given up formal philosophy until the philosophers should once again address themselves to "great issues." While waiting for the change, Gellner was studying the Berbers of Morocco. He visited them now and again and observed their social habits. He considered himself a synoptic thinker — one who saw things as a whole, from the viewpoint of their ultimate significance. He was not a softheaded visionary, and his education at Balliol, traditionally the most rebellious Oxford college, had prepared him to battle with the philosophical Establishment for his unpopular views. He thought that with "Words and Things" he had galvanized men of good sense into taking his side.

Gellner left me reflective. I was sorry that my first philosopher should dislike his colleagues so much. I was sorry, too, that he should turn out to be a harassed man. But then I knew well that prophets are made of strange stuff.

Next day, I walked round to Chelsea to have a talk with Earl Russell at his house. He opened the door himself, and I instantly recognized him as a philosopher by his pipe, which he took out of his mouth to say, "How do you do?" Lord Russell looked very alert. His mop of white hair, swept carelessly back, served as a dignified frame for his learned and animated eyes — eyes that gave life to a wintry face. He showed me into his ground-floor study, which was sandwiched between the garden and the street. It was a snug room, full of books on a large number of subjects: mathematics, logic, philosophy, history, politics. The worn volumes stood as an impressive testament to his changing intellectual interests; they were wedged in with rows of detective stories in glass-fronted Victorian bookcases. "Ah!" he said. "It's just four! I think we can have some tea. I see my good wife has left us some tea leaves." His "ee" sounds were exaggerated. He put a large Victorian kettle on the gas ring. It must have contained little water, for it sang like a choir in a Gothic cathedral. Russell ignored the plainsong and talked, using his pipe, which went out repeatedly, as a baton to lead the conversation. Now and again he reached out to take some tobacco with unsteady fingers from a tin. When we were comfortably settled with our tea, he began interviewing me. Why was I concerned with philosophy when my life was in peril? I should jolly well be doing something about the atomic bomb, to keep the Russians and Americans from sending us all up in flames. Anyone might personally prefer death to slavery, but only a lunatic would think of making this choice for humanity.

At present, when he wasn't working on nuclear disarmament, he used detective stories for an opiate. "I have to read at least one detective book a day," he said, "to drug myself against the nuclear threat." His favorite crime writers were Michael Innes and Agatha Christie. He preferred detective stories to novels because he found that whodunits were more real than howtodoits. The characters in detective stories just did things, but the heroes and heroines in novels thought about things. If you compared sex scenes in the two media, in his sort of pastime they got into and out of bed with alacrity, but in the higher craft the characters were circumspect; they took pages even to sit on the bed. Detective stories were much more lifelike. The paradox was that authors of thrillers did not try to be real, and therefore they were real, while the novelists tried to be real and therefore were unreal. The things we most believed to be unreal — nuclear war — might turn out to be real, and the things we took to be the most real — philosophy — unreal.

The savior in him was eventually tamed by the tea, and the elder statesman of philosophy reminisced a bit about Moore and Wittgenstein, his Cambridge juniors, and said a few caustic words about today's philosophers in Oxford and Cambridge. "I haven't changed my philosophical position for some time," he said. "My model is still mathematics. You see, I started out being a Hegelian. A tidy system it was. Like its child, Communism, it gave answers to all the questions about life and society. In 1898 (how long ago that was!), well, almost everyone seemed to be a Hegelian. Moore was the first to climb down. I simply followed him. It was mathematics that took me to logic, and it was logic that led me away from Hegel. Once we applied rigorous logic to Hegel, he became fragmentary and puerile."

I asked if he had based his system of mathematical logic on the belief that language had a structure.

"No, it is not so much that I believe language has a structure," he said. "I simply think that language is often a rather messy way of expressing things. Take a statement like 'All men are mortal.' Now, that has an unnecessary implication when stated in words; that is, that there are men, that men exist. But if you translate this statement into mathematical symbols, you can do away with any unnecessary implication. About Moore — the thing I remember most was his smile. One had only to see it to melt. He was such a gentleman. With him, manners were everything, and now you know what I mean by 'gentleman.' To be Left, for example, in politics just 'wasn't done.' That was to take something too seriously. I suppose present-day Oxford philosophy is gentlemanly in that sense — it takes nothing seriously. You know the best remark Moore ever made? I asked him one time who his best pupil was, and he said 'Wittgenstein.' I said 'Why?' 'Because, Bertrand, he is my only pupil who always looks puzzled.'" Lord Russell chuckled. "That was such a good remark, such a good remark. It was also, incidentally, very characteristic of both Moore and Wittgenstein. Wittgenstein *was* always puzzled. After Wittgenstein had been my pupil for five terms, he came to me and said, 'Tell me, sir, am I a fool or a wise man?' I said, 'Wittgenstein, why do you want to know?' — perhaps not the kindest thing to say. He said, 'If I am a fool, I shall become an aeronaut — if I am a wise man, a philosopher.' I told him to do a piece of work for me over the vacation, and when he came back I read the first sentence and said, 'Wittgenstein, you shall be a philosopher.' I had to read just a sentence to know it. Wittgenstein became one. When his 'Tractatus' came out, I was wildly excited. I think less well of it now. At that time, his theory that a proposition was a picture of the world was so engaging and original. Wittgenstein was really a Tolstoy and a Pascal rolled into one. You know how fierce Tolstoy was; he hated competitors. If another novelist was held to be better than he, Tolstoy would immediately challenge him to a duel. He did precisely this to Turgenev, and when Tolstoy became a pacifist he was just as fierce about his pacifism. And you know how Pascal became discontented with mathematics and science and became a mystic; it was the same with Wittgenstein. He was a mathematical mystic. But after 'Tractatus' he became more and more remote from me, just like the Oxford philosophers. I have stopped reading Oxford philosophy. I have gone on to other things. It has become so trivial. I don't like most Oxford philosophers. Don't like them. They have made trivial something very great. Don't think much of their apostle Ryle. He's just another clever man. In any case, you have to admit he behaved impetuously in publicly refusing a review of the book. He should have held it over for two years and then printed a short critical review with Gellner's name misspelled. To be a philosopher now, one needs only to be clever. They are all embarrassed when pressed for information, and I am still old-fashioned and like information. Once, I was dining at Oxford — Exeter College High Table — and asked the assembled Fellows what the difference between liberals and conservatives was in their local politics. Well, each of the dons produced brilliant epigrams and it was all very amusing, but after half an hour's recitation I knew no more about liberals and conservatives in the college than I had at the beginning. Oxford philosophy is like that. I have respect for Ayer; he likes information, and he has a first-class style."

Lord Russell explained that he had two models for his own style — Milton's prose and Baedeker's guidebooks. The Puritan never wrote without passion, he said, and the cicerone used only a few words in recommending sights, hotels, and restaurants. Passion was the voice of reason, economy the signature of brilliance. As a young man, Russell wrote with difficulty. Sometimes Milton and Baedeker remained buried in his prose until it had been redone ten times. But then he was consoled by Flaubert's troubles and achievements. Now, for many years past, he had learned to write in his mind, turning phrases, constructing sentences, until in his memory they grew into paragraphs and chapters. Now he seldom changed a word in his dictated manuscript except to slip in a synonym for a word repeated absent-mindedly. "When I was an undergraduate," he said, sucking his pipe, "there were many boys cleverer than I, but I surpassed them, because, while they were *dégagé*, I had passion and fed on controversy. I still thrive on opposition. My grandmother was a woman of caustic and biting wit. When she was eighty-three, she became kind and gentle. I had never found her so reasonable. She noticed the change in herself, and, reading the handwriting on the wall, she said to me, 'Bertie, I'll soon be dead.' And she soon was."

After tea, Lord Russell came to the door with me. I told him about my intention of pressing on with my researches at Oxford. He wrung my hand and chuckled. "Most Oxford philosophers know nothing about science," he said. "Oxford and Cambridge are the last medieval islands — all right for first-class people. But their security is harmful to second-class people — it makes them insular and gaga. This is why English academic life is creative for some but sterile for many."

The Open Door

MY first call in Oxford was at the house of Richard Hare, of Balliol, who, at forty-two, is one of the more influential Oxford teachers of philosophy. His evangelistic zeal for the subject consumes him. He is renowned throughout the university for his kindness, for his selfless teaching, and for writing an exciting book in his field, "The Language of Morals," published in 1952. He is also famous for his eccentric tastes, which I encountered for myself while lunching with him. When I arrived, he was sitting in a caravan — a study on wheels — in the front garden of his house, reading a book. He hailed me from the window, and said, "I find it much easier to work here than in the house. It's quieter, don't you agree?" He looked like a monk, though he wasn't dressed like one; he wore a well-made dark tweed jacket and well-pressed dark-gray flannel trousers — and he had his legendary red and green tie on. After talking for a few minutes through the door of the caravan, we went into the house and joined Mrs. Hare and their four children for lunch. I felt relaxed at his table. His children spoke in whispers and were remarkably well-mannered. His wife was douce and poised. I had been told that invitations to his country-house reading parties during vacations were coveted by able undergraduate philosophers at Oxford, and now I could see why.

At the table, we talked about Hare's interests. "I like music very much — it's one of my principal relaxations," he said at one point. "I listen in a very catholic way to all kinds of music. I deliberately don't have a gramophone, because I think it's better for one to catch what there is on the wireless instead of choosing one's own things. I take in quite a lot of modern stuff, although I don't enjoy it as a whole. I listen to it in the hope that one day I will. Also, on the wireless I have to listen to Beethoven. I'd never go and get a gramophone record of Beethoven. As a schoolboy, I liked him very much, but when the war began I was — as I think most of us were, or anybody at all sensitive — very troubled by war and whether one should be a pacifist. And I can't explain why, but it suddenly became clear to me, listening to Beethoven and to Bach and comparing them, that as *food*, musical food, for anybody in that kind of situation, Beethoven was exceedingly superficial and insipid. But principally superficial. To be precise, it appeared to me one wintry day in 1940 that his music rang exceedingly hollow."

At the end of lunch, Mrs. Hare told us she would

bring us coffee in the caravan, and I followed Hare to his wagon retreat.

I asked him if there was a key to linguistic philosophy.

"No," he said forcefully. "There isn't a method that any fool can get hold of in order to do philosophy as we do it. The most characteristic thing about Oxford philosophy is that we insist on clear thinking, and I suppose scientists and philosophers are agreed on what constitutes a good argument. Clear thinking, of course, is especially important in my own field of moral philosophy, because almost any important moral question arises in a confused form when one first meets it. But most of the undergraduates who come up to Oxford are not going to be professional philosophers; they're going to be civil servants and parsons and politicians and lawyers and businessmen. And I think the most important thing I can do is to teach them to think lucidly — and linguistic analysis is frightfully useful for this. You have only to read the letters to the *Times* — unfortunately I forget them as soon as I've read them, or I'd give you an example — to come across a classic instance of a problem that is made clearer for one, and perhaps would have been made clearer for the writer, by the ability to take statements to pieces. My own hobby is town planning. I read quite a lot of the literature, and it's perfectly obvious that immense harm is done — I mean not just confusion, academic confusion, but physical harm, roads being built in the wrong places and that sort of thing — because people don't think clearly enough. In philosophy itself, unclear thinking has led to a lot of mistakes, and I think it is my job to take pupils through these mistakes and show them the blind alleys in the city of philosophy. They can go on from there. Careful attention to language is, I think, the best way not to solve problems but to understand them. That is what, as philosophers, we are mainly concerned with."

I asked how, exactly, attention to language helped in understanding problems.

"Suppose I said, 'That chair over there is both red and not red,'" he replied. "This would make you say, 'That can't be right.' Well, I say partly it's the same sort of thing that would make you say 'That can't be right' if you wrote down 'fullfil,' spelled f-u-l-l-f-i-l. If you wrote down 'fullfil' that way and you saw it on a page, you would say, 'That can't be right.' Well, this is because you've learned, you see, to do a thing called spelling 'fulfill,' and you've also learned to do a thing called using the word 'not.' And if somebody says to you, 'That is both red and not red,' he's doing something that you learned *not* to do when you learned the word 'not.' He has offended against a certain rule of skill (if you like to call it that), which you mastered when you became aware of how to use the word 'not.' Of course, learning to use the word 'not' isn't exactly like learning how to spell, because it's also knowing something about how to reason. It's mastering a very elementary piece of logic. The words for 'not' in different languages are the same, but not quite the same; there are variations.

For example, in Greek you've double negatives; you say, 'I have not been neither to the temple nor to the theatre.' This is why Oxford philosophy is based both on simple reasoning and on exhaustive research into language — in this particular case, into the word 'not.' "

Hare's ideas about moral philosophy, I learned, were influenced by his experiences in Japanese prison camps in Singapore and Thailand, where all values had to be hewn from the rock of his own conscience. In the artificial community of the prison, he came to realize that nothing was "given" in society, that everyone carried his moral luggage in his head; every man was born with his conscience, and this, rather than anything in society, he found, was the source of morality. (As he once wrote, "A prisoner-of-war community is a society which has to be formed, and constantly re-formed, out of nothing. The social values, whether military or civil, which one has brought with one can seldom be applied without scrutiny to this very strange, constantly disintegrating situation.") Indeed, the rough draft of his first book, "The Language of Morals" — on the strength of which he was eventually elected a Fellow of Balliol — was hammered out in the grim and barren prison compounds. He went on to tell me that his present views, which were a development of his old ideas, were that ethics was the exact study of the words one used in making moral judgments, and that judgment, to be moral, had to be both universal and prescriptive. "This means," he explained, "that if you say 'X ought to do Y,' then you commit yourself to the view that if you were in X's position, you ought to do Y also. Furthermore, if you have said that *you* ought to do Y, then you are bound to do it — straightway, if possible. If you say that X ought to do Y but you don't think that in the same circumstances *you* ought to do it, then it isn't a moral judgment at all." In effect, let your conscience always be your guide. "If you do not assent to the above propositions," Hare went on energetically, "then you do not, in my opinion, really believe in any moral judgments. You cannot answer 'ought'-questions by disguising them as 'is'-questions." He admitted, however, that most of the philosophers at Oxford were not much interested in moral philosophy. For that sort of philosophy one had to go to the Continent and to Existentialism.

What was the relationship between Existentialism and British philosophy?

"The thing wrong with the Existentialists and the other Continental philosophers," Hare said, "is that they haven't had their noses rubbed in the necessity of saying exactly what they mean. I sometimes think it's because they don't have a tutorial system. You see, if you learn philosophy here you read a thing to your tutor and he says to you 'What do you mean by that?' and then you have to tell him. I think what makes us good philosophers is, ultimately, the method of teaching. But you ought to see Iris Murdoch about Existentialism. She's read the big books." He'd read only little Existentialist books, he said. He had no sympathy for people less good than

Miss Murdoch who "let rip on Existentialism and use it as a stick with which to beat 'the sterile Oxford philosophers.'"

Was it possible to be a philosopher and have a religious faith?

Hare pointed out that some of the Oxford philosophers were practicing Christians. He went on to name some Catholics: Elizabeth Anscombe; her husband, Peter Geach (who, though he was not teaching at Oxford, was still "one of us"); B. F. McGuinness; and Michael Dummett. "If you wish to be rational," he went on, "you've got to look for some way of reconciling formal religion, science, and philosophy. I personally think you can reconcile only two of these things. As a philosopher, you can work out your own personal religion, which may or may not conform to what any particular church says, but I think it's slightly sophistical, say, to be a Catholic and then insist that Hell is scientific. Some philosophers here think that they can serve all three masters, and the way they reconcile religion and science is revealing. They take the dogmatic attitude and call it 'empirical': 'When the bad go to Hell, they will *verify* the statement that the bad go to Hell.' So much for the scientific principle of verification! I think if you are a Catholic and are going to be a philosopher, you're almost bound to do one of two things. One is to stick rigidly to the formal kinds of philosophy — I mean mathematical logic, pure linguistic analysis, and that kind of thing. The other is to do ordinary philosophy — my sort — but with a distinct slant."

It was getting late in the afternoon, and I said I must take my leave. We went back into the house, so that I could say goodbye to Mrs. Hare, and she insisted on our taking another cup of coffee. "I hope your afternoon has been worthwhile," she said. "I have learned all the philosophy I know from reading the proofs of my husband's books."

Mr. Hare had been candid and informative. Like all good tutors, he was a little idiosyncratic and somewhat oracular but very approachable.

Next morning, I dropped in on Iris Murdoch. She, Elizabeth Anscombe, and Philippa Foot make up the squadron of Oxford's feminine philosophers, and they and Richard Hare make up the constabulary of moral philosophy at the university. Among her friends and students, Miss Murdoch has the reputation of being a saint, and she has no enemies. She's likely to go about without a thought for her dress and without a penny in her pocket, and this absent-mindedness perhaps has its source in her custom of living and thinking in two worlds — philosophy and literature — both of which she inhabits with facility and aplomb. Two of her engaging novels, "The Bell" and "Under the Net," I had read very recently, and I was surprised that a writer of such gifts should be only a part-time novelist. She greeted me at the door of her study, in Saint Anne's College, and I was immediately drawn to her. She had a striking appearance, very much like my image of St. Joan — a celestial expression cast in the rough features of a peasant, and straight, blond hair unevenly clipped.

I determined to steer my way to philosophy by asking her about her writing. "I do my writing at home, during vacations," she said haltingly. "I settle down with some paper and my characters, and carry on until I get things done. But terms I devote mostly to reading and teaching philosophy — I haven't written any philosophy lately. Yes, I do find time to read a lot of novels, but I don't think I trespass on my serious reading. No, I don't think there is any direct connection between philosophy and my writing. Perhaps they do come together in a general sort of way — in considering, for example, what morality is and what goes into making decisions." She had been an undergraduate at the same time as Hare and, like him, had read Greats, but, unlike him, she had come accidentally to professional philosophy. The aftermath of the war put her in touch with Existentialism. "I was in London during the war," she recalled, "and afterward went to Brussels to do refugee work. In Belgium, there was a tremendous ferment going on; everyone was rushing around reading Kierkegaard and Jean-Paul Sartre. I knew something about them from my undergraduate days, but then I read them deeply." She returned to England and Cambridge to study French philosophy and to look at English philosophy afresh. Wittgenstein had just retired, and she regretted very much that she had arrived too late for his lectures. His philosophy, however, still towered over the university, and she was led up to it by Professor John Wisdom, a disciple of Wittgenstein's, and Miss Anscombe, a pupil and translator of Wittgenstein's, whom Miss Murdoch had known from her undergraduate days.

I asked Miss Murdoch if she had ever seen Wittgenstein.

"Yes. He was very good-looking," she replied, feeling her way like a novelist. "Rather small, and with a very, very intelligent, shortish face and piercing eyes — a sharpish, intent, alert face and those very piercing eyes. He had a trampish sort of appearance. And he had two empty rooms, with no books, and just a couple of deck chairs and, of course, his camp bed. Both he and his setting were very unnerving. His extraordinary directness of approach and the absence of any sort of paraphernalia were the things that unnerved people. I mean, with most people, you meet them in a framework, and there are certain conventions about how you talk to them, and so on. There isn't a naked confrontation of personalities. But Wittgenstein always imposed this confrontation on all his relationships. I met him only twice and I didn't know him well, and perhaps that's why I always thought of him, as a person, with awe and alarm."

She stopped talking suddenly, and it was some time before she resumed. Then she said that she had some things in common, as a moral philosopher, with Miss Anscombe and Mrs. Foot. The three of them were certainly united in their objection to Hare's view that the human being was the monarch of the universe, that he constructed his values from scratch. They were interested in "the reality that surrounds man — transcendent or whatever." She went on to add that the three of them were very dissimilar. "Elizabeth is Catholic and sees God in a particular color," Miss Murdoch said. "Philippa is in the process of changing her position." As for herself, she had not fully worked out her own views, though sometimes she did find herself agreeing with the Existentialists that every person was irremediably different from every other.

Would she perhaps compare the moral philosophy in England and France, I asked, remembering Hare's comment that she had read the big books.

"Some of the French Existentialists feel that certain English philosophers err when they picture morality as a matter of consistency with universal rules," she answered. "The Existentialists think that even though you may endorse the rules society offers you, it is still your own *individual* choice that you endorse them. The Existentialists feel that you can have a morality without producing consistent or explicable rules for your conduct. They allow for a much more personal and aesthetic kind of morality, in which you have to explain yourself, as it were, to your peers."

As she talked on, it became clear to me that she was much more an intuitive person than an analytic one, and regarded ideas as so many precious stones in the human

diadem. Unlike Hare, she found it hard to imagine the
diadem locked up in an ivory tower, or like the Crown
Jewels in the Tower of London. "Most English philosophers," she said, "share certain assumptions of Wittgenstein and Austin. You might want to look into them as
persons. They were the most extraordinary men among
us."

After saying goodbye to Miss Murdoch, I carried my
researches on to Magdalen College. There I intended to
draw out G. J. Warnock, who held one of the keys to the
Austinian legend. This legend was as ubiquitous as the
stained-glass windows, and it might be presumed to il-
luminate the dark room of Oxford philosophy, for J. L.
Austin, who had died a few months before I began my
quest, had dominated Oxford in much the same way that
Wittgenstein had dominated Cambridge. In the course
of an Oxford-to-London telephone call, I asked John,
"What was the source of everyone's veneration of Austin?" and he said, more analytically than unkindly, "Every
cult needs a dead man." He likened the Austinian sect
to primitive Christianity, though he added that he did
not think the worshippers would ever be blessed with
a St. Paul.

As it happened, I had attended one of Austin's lectures, just out of curiosity, while I was an undergraduate,
and had been entranced by his performance. To look
at, he was a tall and thin man, a sort of parody on the
desiccated don. His face suggested an osprey. His

voice was flat and metallic, and seemed to be stuck on a note of disillusion. It sounded like a telephone speaking by itself. The day I was present, he opened his lecture by reading aloud a page from Ayer's "The Problem of Knowledge." He read it in a convincing way, and then he began taking it to bits: "What does he mean by this?" He bore down heavily on Ayer's argument with regard to illusion — that you cannot trust your senses, because they are sometimes mistaken. He said that the passage about people's having illusions made this sound as if it were much more frequent than in fact it was — as if when people saw a stick in water and it looked bent, they were inevitably deceived into thinking that it actually was bent. Austin turned around to the blackboard and, leaning forward, drew a sort of triangle with a thin, crooked stick in it. He added a cherry at the end of the stick. "What is this supposed to be?" he asked, facing us. "A cocktail glass?" And he drew a stem and a foot, asking as he did so, "How many of you think it is a bucket?" He lectured in a deadpan voice, peopling the room with Ayer's deceived men, all of whom would take the glass to be a bucket. This was Austin's way of saying that no more people were deceived by Ayer's stick in the water than by the glass on the blackboard, that Ayer's argument about the fallibility of the senses was much less cogent than he made out, and that most of what the logical positivists called illusions were in fact a madman's delusions. I was told that Austin performed like this day after day, mocking, ridiculing, caricaturing, exaggerating, never flagging in his work of demolition, while the skeptical undergraduates watched, amused and bemused, for behind the performance — the legend — there was the voice of distilled intelligence. Austin's trenchant remarks on philosophers would make a small volume of cherished quotations, and among them would surely be a clerihew he wrote on the Harvard logician W. V. Quine:

> Everything done by Quine
> Is just fine.
> All we want is to be left alone,
> To fossick around on our own.

When I arrived at Magdalen, I found Warnock reading the bulletin board in the porter's lodge. He looked slightly younger than Hare, and was round-faced and rather tweedy; his appearance went with round-rimmed glasses, though he didn't have any glasses on. He was, however, wearing a rather nice, formal V-shaped smile. Yes, he was expecting me, he said, and took me straight to the Senior Common Room for lunch. Warnock was the custodian of Austin's papers, but we didn't talk about Austin right away. Once we were in the S.C.R., I asked him about the lightning attack he and Dr. David Pears, of Christ Church College, had made on Gellner and Watkins in a discussion on the B.B.C. Third Programme in 1957. After Gellner's polemical book appeared, some of his detractors had claimed that this broadcast had provided him with both the motive and the cue for writing it — that when the articulate Oxford pair defeated the less articulate Gellner and his satellite, Watkins, the defeat had made Watkins sulk and Gellner write. "I wish I'd known that that little rapping of the knuckles would lead to the big storm," Warnock said. "Gellner is a rather sensitive chap." I had not expected him to show even this much sympathy for Gellner, for I had been told that Warnock was one of Austin's two or three favorites, and I knew Austin was one of Gellner's main targets.

The lunch was a communal affair, an occasion for general conversation, and I was not able to draw Warnock out until it was time for coffee, when all the other Fellows settled down to their newspapers and we managed to find a corner to ourselves. Once I had mentioned Austin, Warnock needed no further urging. I just sat back and listened.

"Like Wittgenstein," he said, "Austin was a genius, but Wittgenstein fitted the popular picture of a genius. Austin, unfortunately, did not. Nevertheless, he did succeed in haunting most of the philosophers in England, and to his colleagues it seemed that his terrifying intelligence was never at rest. Many of them used to wake up in the night with a vision of the stringy, wiry Austin standing over their pillow like a bird of prey. Their daylight hours were no better. They would write some philosophical sentences and then read them over as Austin might, in an expressionless, frigid voice, and their blood would run cold. Some of them were so intimidated by the mere fact of his existence that they weren't able to publish a single article during his lifetime."

Austin's all-consuming passion was language, Warnock went on, and he was endlessly fond of reading books on grammar. He thought of words as if they were insects, which needed to be grouped, classified, and labelled, and just as the entomologist was not put off by the fact that there were countless insects, so the existence of thousands of words, Austin thought, should not be a deterrent to a lexicographer-philosopher. "Austin," Warnock said, "wanted philosophers to classify these 'speech acts' — these promises, prayers, hopes, commendations." In Austin's view, most philosophers in the past had stumbled on some original ideas and had spent their time producing a few illustrative examples for their theories, and then as soon as they were safely dead other philosophers would repeat the process with slightly different original ideas. This practice had frozen philosophy from the beginning of time into an unscientific, noncumulative state. Austin wanted to thaw the ice of ages, by unflagging application of the intellect, and make philosophy a cumulative science, thus enabling one philosopher to pick up where his predecessor had left off. "He envisaged the future task of philosophers as the compilation of a super-grammar — a catalogue of all possible functions of words — and this was perhaps why he enjoyed reading grammar books so much," Warnock said. "He was extremely rigid in pursuit of details, and he had the patience and efficiency needed for this difficult task. If he had not died at forty-eight — he had cancer, you know — his detailed work might have led to some beautiful things."

"Was Austin influenced by Wittgenstein?" I asked.

"Oh, no," Warnock said quickly. "In all of Austin's papers there is no evidence that he ever really read him. I do remember one or two of his lectures in which he read a page or two of Wittgenstein aloud, but it was always to show how incomprehensible and obscure the Austrian philosopher was, and how easily he could be parodied and dismissed."

I was getting worried by the fact that I was supposed to admire Austin as a man, and said, "Were there some things about him that were human?"

"Oh, yes," said Warnock, with a smile that indicated a faint donnish disapproval of my question. "He was one of the best teachers here. He taught us all absolute accuracy."

I repeated my question in a slightly different form.

"He really was a very unhappy man," Warnock said quietly. "It worried him that he hadn't written much. One lecture, 'Ifs and Cans,' which appeared in the *Proceedings of the British Academy* in 1956, became famous, but it is mainly a negative work, and he published very few articles and, significantly, not a single book. He read, of course — an enormous amount — and the margins of everything he went over were filled with notes, queries, and condemnations. When he went to Harvard to give the William James lectures, in 1955, he took everyone there by surprise. Because he hadn't written anything, they expected his lectures to be *thin*, for they judged the worth of scholars according to their *big books*.

From his very first lecture they realized that his reading was staggering. To add to his writing block, he had a fear of microphones, and this prevented him from broadcasting, like Sir Isaiah Berlin; this was another source of unhappiness. He took enormous pride in teaching, but this began to peter out in his last years, when he felt that he had reached the summit of his influence at Oxford. Toward the end of his life, therefore, he decided to pack up and go permanently to the University of California in Berkeley, where he had once been a visiting professor and where he thought he'd have more influence as a teacher. But before he could get away from Oxford, he died."

Warnock was in the middle of straightening out and editing Austin's papers, and he told me there were scores of bad undergraduate essays that Austin had written for his tutor at Balliol. "These essays were of little value because his philosophy tutor set him useless subjects," Warnock said. It was probably his education at his public school, Shrewsbury, rather than at Balliol, that got him his Firsts, the Magdalen tutor thought. Besides the bad essays, his papers included only two sets of lectures — one on perception, the other the William James addresses. But both of them were in note form, and would not total much more than eighty thousand words when Warnock had finished turning them into sentences. Warnock was worried by his task of filling out his master's lectures. If, by some miracle, the Austin-Warnock composition did add up to a hundred thousand words, then the publishers might be persuaded to bring out the work in two handsome volumes. Otherwise, there would be only one posthumous book, along with the few published articles, as a record of Austin's genius. (Some time later, the Oxford University Press brought out a small book, "Sense and Sensibilia," by Austin, reconstructed from manuscript notes by Warnock.) There were, of course, his many devoted pupils, and *they* would commemorate him.

Austin's family life, I learned, had been conventional. "He married a pupil, and had four children," Warnock said. "He was a good husband and a good father. His daughter, now eighteen, is about to come up to Oxford; his elder son, who is seventeen, is going to do engineering. The third child, a boy of fourteen, is very clever, and is about to go up to my school, Winchester. He talks and looks very much like Austin, and we have great hopes for him. The youngest child is a girl."

It was time to go, and as Warnock walked out to the porter's lodge with me, I asked him a bit about himself. Unlike most of the other philosophers about, he had not read Greats straightway. He had done P.P.E. — a combination of modern philosophy, political science, and economics — before going on to a year of Greats and a prize fellowship at Magdalen. He had been very fortunate in having Sir Isaiah Berlin, now Chichele Professor of Social and Political Theory, for his tutor, and also in having a philosopher for his wife. She and Warnock had together managed the Jowett Society (for undergraduate philosophers), and they had decided to get married after they were officers emeritus. He was writing a book on free will — one of the oldest chestnuts in the philosophical fire. His parting injunction to me was to see Strawson. "He'll be able to tell you some more about Austin," he called after me, waving.

I walked back to my old college, where I'd been given a guest room, to pick up my mail, and was delighted to find a letter from John, who had an uncanny gift of never failing me; he seemed to sense my questions before I could put them. Just as Oxford philosophy, in his words, "made a technique of being non-technical," John made a technique of helping his friends without apparent effort. It cheered me up to find out that his impatience with philosophy did not extend to his friend's researches. He said that I shouldn't miss seeing Strawson. "He not only is the best philosopher in the university but is also unrivalled as a teacher of it," John wrote. "He's discovering new stars in the philosophical firmament." Austin, he went on, had his equal in Strawson; indeed, at one meeting of the exclusive Aristotelian Society, *crème de la crème* of all philosophical societies, Strawson had roundly defeated Austin in a disputation about Truth — a truth that Austin had never acknowledged.

Next day, I waited for P. F. Strawson, Fellow of University College, Oxford, in his Senior Common Room. Strawson, who is considered by both undergraduates and his colleagues to be the most high-powered and creative philosopher in England, arrived just a little late and greeted me apologetically. He had blue eyes with what I took to be a permanently worried expression, and, at forty-one, looked like an elderly young man. At lunch, I asked him to tell me a little bit about himself, which he did, in a modest fashion that by now I had stopped associating with philosophers. He had been schooled in Finchley, a suburb of London, he said, and he had read Greats about the same time as Hare, Miss Murdoch, Miss Anscombe, Warnock. His career, like theirs, had been interrupted by the war, the close of which found him teaching in Wales. "I didn't know what provincialism was until I got there," he said. He had been delighted to get an appointment to Oxford, partly because Oxford had more philosophy in its curriculum than any other university. This, he explained, was the reason that a philosophy planted in Cambridge had flowered at Oxford. Cambridge now had only two eminent philosophers — John Wisdom and R. B. Braithwaite — while Oxford was swarming with them. Without the buzz-buzz, there would be no philosophy, he said; the university would be a hive minus the honey.

After lunch, as I climbed up the steps to his room, I felt I was leaving the Oxford of lost causes behind me — the way he moved suggested subdued confidence. We sat by the window, and for some time, as we talked, I was aware of the acrobatic motions of Strawson's legs, which were now wrapped around one of the legs of a writing table and now slung over another chair.

We talked about other philosophers as so many birds outside preying on the insects that Austin had dug up for them. I felt I'd reached the augur of philosophy. On the window sill were lying the proofs of an article called "Philosophy in England," which was stamped *"Times Literary Supplement,* Special Issue on the British Imagination." Strawson admitted that he was the author of the anonymous piece, and while he went to telephone for some coffee, I glanced, with his permission, at the first paragraph:

An Australian philosopher, returning in 1960 to the center of English philosophy after an absence of more than a decade, remarked on, and regretted, the change he found. He had left a revolutionary situation in which every new move was delightfully subversive and liberating. He returned to find that, though the subject appeared still to be confidently and energetically cultivated, the revolutionary ferment had quite subsided. Where there had been, it seemed to him, a general and triumphant movement in one direction, there were now a number of individuals and groups pursuing divergent interests and ends, often in a relatively traditional manner.

When Strawson had returned to his chair, I asked him whether he agreed with the Australian philosopher. He said he did — that "the view of the Australian philosopher was essentially right." For a fuller statement of his own conclusions, he modestly directed me to the summary at the end of his article:

Even in the heyday of the linguistic movement, it is doubtful whether it numbered among its adherents or semi-adherents more than a substantial minority of British philosophers.

It was associated primarily with one place — Oxford — and there it centered around one man — Austin — its most explicit advocate and most acute and wholehearted practitioner. Its heyday was short. When a revolutionary movement begins to write its own history, something at least of its revolutionary impetus has been lost; and in the appearance of "The Revolution in Philosophy" [by A. J. Ayer, W. C. Kneale, G. A. Paul, D. F. Pears, P. F. Strawson, G. J. Warnock, and R. A. Wollheim, with an introduction by Gilbert Ryle, 1956] . . . and of G. J. Warnock's "English Philosophy since 1900" (1958) there were signs that eyes were being lifted from the immediate task, indications of pause and change. Indeed, the pull of generality was felt by Austin himself, who, before he died, was beginning to work out a general classificatory theory of acts of linguistic communication. It is still too early to say what definite directions change will take. In spite of the work of Ayer, who never attached value to the linguistic idea, and who, in his most recent book, "The Problem of Knowledge" (1956), continued to uphold a traditional empiricism with unfailing elegance and skill, it seems unlikely that he or others will work much longer in the vein. There are portents, however, of a very different kind. One is the appearance of a persuasive study entitled "Hegel: A Re-examination" (1958), by J. N. Findlay. Hampshire's "Thought and Action" (1959), with its linking of epistemology, philosophy of mind, and moral philosophy, is highly indicative of a trend from piecemeal studies towards bolder syntheses; it shows how the results of recent discussions can be utilized in a construction with both Hegelian and Spinozistic affinities. Strawson's "Individuals" (1959) suggests a scaled-down Kantianism, pared of idealism on the one hand and a particular conception of physical science on the other. The philosophy of logic and language takes on a tauter line and a more formal tone in the work of logicians who derive their inspiration mainly from Frege. Finally, some of the most successful work of the period has been in the philosophy of mind; and it seems reasonable to suppose that further studies will follow upon Ryle's "Concept of Mind" (1949), Wittgenstein's "Investigations" (1953), and Miss Anscombe's "Intention" (1957) and that, in them, Ryle's explicit and Wittgenstein's implicit suggestions of systematization will be refined and reassessed. The Australian philosopher had reason enough to claim that he found a changed situation. When knowledge of this fact of change finally filters through to those who habitually comment on the state of philosophy without any significant first-hand acquaintance with it, reactions of complacency may be expected. In the anticipated face of these it is worth reaffirming that the gains and advances made in the dozen years which followed the war were probably as great as any which have been made in an equivalent period in the history of the subject. A new level of refinement and accuracy in conceptual awareness has been reached, and an addition to philosophical method has been established which will, or should, be permanent.

I wanted my augur to divine in more detail the flights of the philosophical birds, and asked him to tell me what was next.

"Fifteen years ago," he began, with a nod to the past, "we were perhaps over-confident, and dismissed the problems of the great thinkers of the past as mere verbal confusions. It was right after the war, and we were mesmerized by Wittgenstein and Austin." Some were still under their spell, he continued, but within the last five years most had wandered out of the magic circle.

"Was the Russell and Gellner charge of sterility in

philosophy applicable, then, only to the first decade after the war?" I asked.

He thought so, he said, adding, "They are thinking of things like Austin's Saturday mornings." He went on to tell me that these meetings admitted only Fellows, no professors or others senior to Austin. Austin and his pet colleagues whiled away their Saturday mornings by distinguishing shades of meaning and the exact applications of words like "rules," "regulations," "principles," "maxims," "laws." "Even this method, sterile with anyone else, was very fertile with Austin," Strawson said, "though apparently not for Sir Isaiah Berlin and Stuart Hampshire. Sir Isaiah didn't last very long, because the whole approach was uncongenial to him, and in any case his genius lay in breathing life into the history of ideas. Most of the other brilliant philosophers, however, turned up regularly." This was perhaps what gave Oxford philosophy some sort of unity in the eyes of its critics, Strawson thought, but they overlooked the fact that on weekdays Austin did encourage (with results) people to do research in perception — in psychology and physiology. "Even on his Saturday mornings, toward the end of his life, he was coming around to more general sorts of questions," Strawson added, waggling his feet on the table. He then echoed a sentiment I'd heard again and again at Oxford: "Austin was one of the kindest men in the university." He went on, "As for the present, we are now rediscovering our way to the traditional way of doing philosophy. Ryle is composing a book on Plato and Aristotle, Warnock is reworking the problem of free will, and I'm writing a little volume on Kant." Thus, everything was now in ferment, and he imagined that the future might hold a philosophical synthesis chiselled and shaped with linguistic tools.

Strawson's scout brought in some coffee, and both of us sipped it gratefully. I spent the remaining time piecing together Strawson's intellectual biography. He spent the early fifties writing "Introduction to Logical Theory," in which he tried to explode Russell's theory that formal logic was the road to a perfect, unmessy language. Logic was simple and ordinary language was complex, Strawson maintained in this work, and therefore neither could supplant the other. But it was really his "Individuals," published in 1959, that contained his present views. He devoted the second half of the fifties to working out the distinctions presented in "Individuals." "In my 'Individuals,'" he said, "instead of analyzing the language, I ask what the necessary *conditions* of language are. Like Kant, I reach the conclusion that objects exist in space and time, and that our language is derived from *them*, rather than the objects from the language. This enables me to state that the concept of a person *precedes* the idea of mind and body — that we think of a person, which includes mind and body, *before* we think of either mind or body. Through this concept of persons I solve the old dualistic problem — how mind and body, if two separate entities, can interact on each other. I answer that I can think of myself as an *objective* person — which subsumes both mind and body — when I postulate the existence of other persons. In my view, people's existence is objective in the same sense that, for example, this table is hard. It is hard because everyone agrees that it is hard, and it does not make any sense to say 'This is not so,' or to ask whether it is really hard. But if everyone had a different opinion about whether this table was hard or not, the fact of the table's hardness would, for that very reason, cease to be objective, and one would have to speak in some such terms as 'I have the peculiar sense of this table.' If people had peculiar senses of the table, it would deprive the table of existence. This argument holds for existence generally. For the existence of anything would be a private experience if people didn't agree about it. In my 'Individuals' I establish that agreement about the hard table is tantamount to saying that the table exists. But the sort of objectivity we ascribe to the hard table we cannot quite ascribe to pain, for example, because people do not agree about other people's pain, and people do not feel pain all at the same time. If they did, we should be able to talk about pain in the same way that we talk about the hard table. Nonetheless, I am able to establish that pain is objective."

By now, his legs were completely entangled with those of the hard table, but it was quite clear to me that he was one thing and the hard table another, and that both of them (hard table more than he) were objective. It was also quite clear to me that if men were no longer just clockwork machines, or Pavlov's dogs with ivory-tower bells ringing for their intellectual food, then metaphysics (or the mind) — which until the publication of Strawson's "Individuals" Oxford philosophers thought they had discarded forever — was now back in the picture. With the edifying thought that I had a mind in some sense as objective as my body, I took my leave of the scaled-down Kant.

I returned to my college and found John in its buttery; he had come up to consult some classical manuscripts in the Bodleian Library. Once beer was served, we settled down on a bench in a corner.

"I don't really want to talk *your* subject," John said, smiling, "but my curiosity has got the better of me."

"I've just come from Strawson," I said. "He explained to me his notions about mind and body, but I did find them difficult. What do you think about them?"

"As I told you in London," he began, reluctantly but good-humoredly, "I only skimmed the second half of 'Individuals.' "

"Yes, yes," I said. "Go on."

"The ideas contained in 'Individuals' have a very long history," John said. "Without going into all of it, you know that in the thirties Wittgenstein talked a lot about the problem of mind and body. His pupils kept elaborate authorized notes, which were only recently published as 'The Blue and Brown Books.' It was during his lifetime that Ryle brought out his 'The Concept of Mind,' which galled Wittgenstein very much, since it contained many of his unpublished ideas. Ryle had reached most of his conclusions independently, but this did not assuage old Wittgenstein, who had allowed himself to be beaten at the publishing game."

John swallowed some beer and then fumbled in several pockets for tobacco, pipe cleaner, and matches. As he filled his pipe, he blew a question in my direction: "Would you like to know something about 'The Concept of Mind'?"

I said I would, especially since Ryle, for personal reasons, was unable to see me. "Well, it is a great work and has had enormous influence," John said. "In this book, Ryle talks about the question 'What is knowledge?' and also talks, more significantly, about what he calls, or, rather, what he caricatures as, 'the dogma of the Ghost in the Machine.'" The behaviorists, he went on to explain, had maintained that there was no mind but only a body — Pavlov's dogs — and that all statements supposedly about the mind were covertly about the body. For them, thinking came down to merely a movement of the larynx, for when you think you can feel your throat move, as if you were talking to yourself. Ryle became convinced that the behaviorists had not conquered the classic problem of the mind and the body, and went on to ask the classic question of how one gets from the mind to the body — how the two halves meet. When I feel a pain, how do I get, say, from the pinched nerve ends to sensing a pain; or when I am revolted by a bad smell, how does, say, the sulphur applied to my nostrils find its way to the inside of my mind? In "The Concept of Mind," Ryle, like the behaviorists, dismissed the commonly held theory, formulated by Descartes, among others, that the human person consists of two halves, the mind and the body, the body being material, or visible, audible, tastable, touchable, and smellable, and the mind being spiritual, or invisible, inaudible, untastable, untouchable, and unsmellable. He caricatured this dualism as the Ghost in the Machine. The Ghost-in-the-Machine men thought that when one said "I feel a pain" or "I see a flash," one was referring to a private mental act; such acts, unlike the movements of the body, were not verifiable except by the person who performed them. "Ryle, agreeing with the behaviorists, said that in fact we know perfectly well whether other people want things and hate things and know things," John continued. "You tell whether someone knows something by his actions. If I say 'I know how to read,' this doesn't say anything about the private state of my mind, invisible, inaudible, and so on, but just means that if you put a book in front of me I can read it. That kind of thing. There's a whole series of potential statements that can thus be 'unpacked' — Ryle's expression — at will. Ryle reached the triumphant conclusion that there are not two parts to the person but, rather, one entity, which is — well, it's not just body. This conclusion is not quite behaviorism — which doesn't recognize any mind — but posits a machine with a plus. As always, though, various people were soon as dissatisfied with Ryle as he had been with the behaviorists, and as the behaviorists had been with Descartes' Ghost-in-the-Machine man. For my part, I've never been very clear what's supposed to be wrong with 'The Concept of Mind,' except that I myself do believe that there is a ghost in the machine and I do not see how you can get on without one. I realize that this attitude is disreputable. I mean *absolutely* disreputable, not just unprofessional, for *today* my belief would be considered full of logical lacunae."

Because I wanted John to make a connection between Ryle and Strawson before I lost "The Concept" in the philosophical fog in my mind, I didn't pause to commiserate with him but pressed on. "How does Strawson improve on Ryle?" I asked.

"Strawson is very good in this, because he tries to preserve something from Descartes, on the one hand, and behaviorism revised by Ryle, on the other," John said. "He says that you can't understand the meaning of the word 'thinking' unless you can understand both its mental and its physical aspects. Take pain, for example. Descartes would have said that pain was only a mental occurrence; the behaviorists, with modifications from Ryle, said that pain was mere physical behavior — hopping up and down and going 'Ow!' or something like that. But Strawson says that you can't understand the word 'pain' unless you understand both its aspects: (1) the hopping around and (2) the feeling of pain; and that since *both* other people and I hop around when we are in pain, and since *both* also feel it, pain is checkable, is, in a way, objective. Thus, by including both these aspects in the concept of 'persons' (which in turn includes one-self and other people), he is able to add further pluses to the old machine. Strawson's on to something new, but all the philosophers here are niggling at one or two logical flaws in his chapter on persons, because most of them still tend to cling to behaviorism. There's one chap who carries behaviorism to such an extreme that he says that even to dream is merely to acquire a disposition to tell stories in the morning."

John rose to go. "I must get to the Bodleian before it closes," he said.

"One or two minutes more, John," I begged, and he accepted another half pint.

John told me a few things about Ryle. He came from a family of clerical dignitaries, and this probably explained his anticlericalism. He was educated in a "marginal public school" and at Queen's College, Oxford. He read both Greats and P.P.E., with enormous success, and managed at the same time to be on the rowing crew. The Senior Common Room atmosphere — any Common Room would do — fitted him like a glove. He essentially liked drinking beer with his fellow-men. He pretended to dislike intellectual matters and publicized his distaste for reading, but he had been known to reveal encyclopedic knowledge of Fielding and Jane Austen. He loved gardening, and he also loved going to philosophical conventions, where his charm overwhelmed everyone. Young philosophers swarmed round him and he was too kind to them. He was a perfect Victorian gentleman; he would have been a sitting duck for Matthew Arnold's criticism of Philistinism, just as he actually was for Gellner's attack on idle philosophy. "Once, Ryle saw Isaiah Berlin coming from a performance of Bach's B-Minor Mass in the Sheldonian Theatre," John said. "Berlin was totally absorbed by the moving experience he had just undergone. Ryle shouted to him across Broad Street, 'Isaiah, have you been listening to some tunes again?'"

John put down his mug and stood up. "I really must go," he said. "I hope you won't assume from my hasty picture of Ryle that I don't like him. Actually, he's a very lovable man, and a highly intelligent one. I simply don't share his distrust of imagination. You know, Hume devoted very little space in all his works to the imagination. He said that it was only a peculiar faculty of mind that could combine primary experiences, enabling one to picture centaurs and mermaids. Well, Ryle has very much the same conception. His own images are mundane, like so many gateposts, firm in the ground." John waved and departed.

My next call was at Professor Ayer's rooms, in New College. He was sitting at his desk, writing, and after he had risen to greet me, he said, rather grandly, "Would you terribly mind waiting a bit? I'm just writing the last paragraph of my address." His professorship at Oxford was recent, and he still had to deliver his public inaugural lecture. I sat down across from the philosopher at work. His whole appearance was very striking. He was a rather small man, with a fine, triangular face and a slightly hooked nose. His curly hair, turning silver gray, was beautifully brushed; he seemed to have just come out of a barbershop, and had a sort of glamorous sheen that I had not theretofore met up with among the philosophers. He was smoking not a pipe but a cigarette, in a long holder. And now, instead of writing, he was leaning back in his chair and impatiently twisting his hands. He looked rather self-consciously thoughtful. Then he leaned forward and started writing rapidly, and a few moments later he laid down his pen. "There!" he exclaimed. "I have written my last sentence." Talking in a somewhat birdlike voice, he explained that his lecture surveyed postwar philosophy in England and interpreted the philosophical handwriting on the wall. If one thought of philosophers as idealists and realists, the idealists were out — had been since the demise of Josiah Royce (1916) and F. H. Bradley (1924). The army of philosophers thus lacked a soft, or idealist, wing, though it did have marginal people like Hare, Foot, and Anscombe. Its tough wing was made up of Wittgenstein, Wisdom, Austin, Ryle, Strawson, and Ayer himself, with his logical positivism. "But then," Ayer chirped, "it's very unprofessional to talk about philosophers as tough or tender, dry or wet. The whole idea is quite absurd, quite absurd." He would leave all that out of his final draft, he said.

We had a quick drink and then walked out of his beautiful college and up Catte Street and down the High to the Mitre Hotel for some dinner. On the way, I told Ayer which philosophers I had met. "A very good selection it is, too," he said. "Hampshire is the only other one I wouldn't miss if I were you." Hampshire had left Oxford to take Ayer's former chair at London University. "Why don't you catch the train with me to London this evening?" Ayer suggested. "I honestly think more Oxford philosophers will simply mix you up."

I said I would think about it over dinner.

We were soon dining, and during the meal I learned something about Ayer. Like the great Berlin, he was born of foreign parentage — his mother was Dutch, his father French-Swiss — and the father, like Berlin's, had been a timber merchant. "Though Isaiah's father was a successful timber merchant, mine wasn't," he added, playing with a silver watch chain and smiling. Ayer had been a scholar at Eton. He had come up to Christ Church in 1929; most of his Oxford contemporaries were rather undistinguished and had been forgotten. "It wasn't like the late thirties, which were really the vintage years of undergraduates," Ayer explained. "Oxford owes many of its great philosophers to the prewar harvest. Some of my friends, post-university acquisitions, are Left Wing playwrights and novelists — I mean people like John Osborne, Kingsley Amis, and John Wain. I just like their society and their way of living, and perhaps this explains why I find London much more exciting than Oxford — also, incidentally, why people sometimes connect me with the so-called Left Wing Establishment. As for my inter-

ests, I rather like rereading old novels. I only go through
the new ones when they're written by people I know. I
love being on television and I love watching it, and I do
think the B.B.C. is a wonderful institution. They used to
invite me at least once every six weeks to lecture or to
appear on the intellectual discussion program, 'The
Brains Trust,' and they show those wonderful Westerns
and programs like 'Panorama' and 'Tonight.' Both my
stepdaughter, Gully, and I enjoy them very much. I
actually don't think my television discussions interfere
with my philosophy, because if I consistently worked
a four-hour day on my subject I could produce a philosophical work every six months. Though I came to
philosophy from Greats, as almost everyone here did
— for that matter, all recent English philosophers except
Russell, Wittgenstein, and Strawson were first Greek
and Latin scholars — language qua language has never
been a great passion of mine. This makes me temperamentally closer to Russell than to anybody else, and
probably rather a freak at Oxford."

By the end of dinner, I had decided to catch the train
with Ayer. He had a first-class return ticket, so I joined
him, and we had a big carriage to ourselves. He pulled
Amis's "Take a Girl Like You" out of his briefcase and
laid it beside him, and then he put his legs up on the seat
opposite and asked me, with a little smile, if I had any
burning philosophical puzzles.

I said I really felt I was steaming away from the subject, but perhaps he could separate Wittgenstein and

Austin for me, since they had now got linked in my mind like Siamese twins.

"Wittgenstein was interested in fundamental philosophical problems, Austin in language for its own sake," Ayer said. "Yet Austin, despite Gellner, was not a linguist, in any ordinary sense of the word; he was not interested in etymology or in the growth of language. He applied himself only to the function of words." He agreed that there was some truth in the view that philosophy for Austin was an impersonal investigation but for Wittgenstein was intensely personal. Indeed, Wittgenstein thought of himself as a living philosophical problem. "I think that before you finish your researches, you ought to read Norman Malcolm's memoir of Wittgenstein," Ayer said. "The book is in a sense a piece of destructive hagiography; the genre is hardly a model for anyone — in any case, it's not well written — but it does incidentally reveal a few things about the saint of postwar philosophy." Ayer also said that Wittgenstein often made friends not because of their intellectual gifts but because of their moral qualities, so that some of the stories passed around about him were a little fuzzy. Until the middle thirties little was known about Wittgenstein's ideas outside Cambridge, for to give his teaching continuity he preferred the same band of disciples year after year. And although some of his students' lecture notes were authorized and circulated, his ideas of the thirties were available only to the elect until the posthumous publication of his "Blue and Brown Books." Wittgenstein's pupils were very remarkable for their intelligence and sometimes for their reproduction of the Master's mannerisms. His eccentricity was contagious, and few people came in contact with him without acquiring a touch of his habits, which fitted him, as a genius, but did not always suit others, who were just great intellectuals. His most conspicuously distinguished pupil was Wisdom but the closest to him was Miss Anscombe, whose brilliant translations of his German works would have been enough in themselves to earn her a place in the English pantheon of philosophers. Wittgenstein had a pathological fear that his ideas would be perverted by anyone who did not understand them fully. Although Ayer had never been a pupil of Wittgenstein's, once he had pieced together a statement of Wittgenstein's current ideas and published it in *Polemic* in the forties. This had enraged the Cambridge philosopher, and for a while he showed a snarling hostility. "He had that side to his character also," Ayer said.

Ayer picked up "Take a Girl Like You" and started leafing through it. "I don't really think it's as good as 'Lucky Jim,'" he said. "In its way, that was a first-rate work." The train was jerkily jogging its way through the night. A look out the window was drowsy-making, but Ayer seemed very fresh.

I racked my sleepy brain for some more questions, and finally asked him whether there was one particular quality that all philosophers shared.

He was thoughtful for a moment and then said,

"Vanity. Yes, vanity is the *sine qua non* of philosophers. In the sciences, you see, there are established criteria of truth and falsehood. In philosophy, except where questions of formal logic are involved, there are none, and so the practitioners are extremely reluctant to admit error. To come back to Austin, no one would deny the incisive quality of his mind, and yet when Strawson defeated him in an argument about Truth, it never seemed to have once crossed Austin's mind that he was the vanquished. To take another example, Russell attacks Strawson as though he were just another Oxford philosopher, without reading him carefully. But perhaps at his age Russell has a right to make up his mind about a book without reading it." Some of the philosophers were vain not only about their thoughts but about their personal influence, Ayer added. Wittgenstein dominated his classes, and, of course, Austin was an absolute dictator at his Saturday mornings.

"Is there anything like those groups now?" I asked.

"Well, I've just organized one," Ayer said. "We meet Thursday evenings, but I hope we do things in a more relaxed way than either Austin or Wittgenstein did." His Thursday meetings were very informal, he explained. There was no preordained leader, but to make the discussion effective only a handful of philosophers were allowed to join in. Disputation took place after dinner over whiskey or beer, and it centered on one subject, chosen for the term. The topic for the next term was "Time." " 'Truth' may be going out," Ayer said, "but 'Time' is coming back into the philosophical purview."

"What is the spread of Oxford philosophy?" I asked. "Is it practiced far and wide?"

"There are some exceptions, but I should say that you find at Oxford a fair representation of the kinds of philosophy that are studied in England, for the simple reason that Oxford staffs other universities with philosophers," Ayer said. "The real spread of Austin's linguistic philosophy is in the Dominions and the United States. For this, Ryle must take some of the responsibility. He likes Dominion and American students, and some people feel that he admits too many of them to Oxford for postgraduate work. Most students arrive already intoxicated with the idea of linguistic philosophy, but they soon find the scene much more diversified than they had expected. Not all of them profit by the discovery. So, many return to their countries to practice Austin's methods wholesale. The first-rate people in America, like W. V. Quine, at Harvard, and Ernest Nagel, at Columbia, and Nelson Goodman, at Pennsylvania, don't give a curse for Oxford philosophy, but I should imagine there are more second-rate people doing linguistic analysis in America than in England and the Dominions put together."

We pulled into the Paddington station and, taking separate taxis, closed the philosophers' shop for the night.

I spent that night at John's. He was in bed when I arrived, and he had left for the British Museum library when I woke up, so I didn't get a chance to talk to him until the middle of the afternoon, when he returned from the Museum to make himself a sardine sandwich.

"What's on your philosophical agenda?" he asked, between bites.

"I'm having a drink with Hampshire," I said.

"You'll like him very much," John said. "He's still the idol of all the young Fellows of All Souls, where he spent many years before coming to London." He added that Hampshire was a great figure, who was not only still admired by All Souls men but looked up to by the whole of Oxford. This I could easily believe, because I remembered how highly he had been regarded in my own undergraduate days. He had also been passionate about Socialism in a youthful kind of way, which had made the undergraduate societies court him as an after-dinner speaker. Intelligent Oxford — at least, since the thirties — was Left Wing, and he had been a patron saint of the politically conscious university. His beliefs were reasoned, and he was emotionally committed to his ideas — a rare thing for an Oxford philosopher — and because his convictions were a matter of the heart as well as of the head, he had the rare ability to electrify clubs and societies. He might share his politics with Ayer, but Ayer had only recently returned to Oxford; besides, Ayer's Socialism was perhaps a little remote.

I asked John what he recalled about Hampshire.

"Well," he said, "as you probably know, he was a star pupil at his school — Repton — and was very much under the influence of one of its masters. Hampshire inherited his liberal principles from his mentor. Sometime in the early thirties, he came up to Balliol, where he fortified his Leftist views with wider reading. The last year of the war found him in the Foreign Office, and they didn't know what to make of him, because he used to start discussions by saying, 'The first thing to do is to find out if our foreign policy is Socialistic.' Hampshire claimed he started doing philosophy because he liked to argue, but in fact he avoided philosophical arguments."

Leaving John, I taxied to University College (this time, of London University), and found Professor Hampshire standing on the steps of the building where he had his office. His hands were clasped rather boyishly behind his back, and his curly blond hair was flying in the wind. "Hello!" he called. "I've just locked myself out of the office." He looked at me expectantly, as though I might have brought him the key. Taking hold of the handle of the door, he shook it vigorously and waited in vain for it to spring open. "I like the Oxford system of not locking doors," he said. "This sort of thing would never have happened to me there. There isn't a pub for some stretch." Nevertheless, we started in search of one. We came upon a Lyons Corner House, and ducked in for some tea, because Hampshire was thirsty. Sitting down, he surveyed the motley tea drinkers in the room and said, "This is what I like about London. You always feel close to the people." But the clatter and noise of Hampshire's people were so deafening that we were soon driven out.

We finally spotted a pub. When we had settled down in it, I asked him about his latest book, "Thought and Action."

"I'm not very good at summing up my own arguments,"

he said. "But my view of philosophy couldn't be further from Austin's. Like the ancient philosophers, I feel our function is really to advance opinions, and I think philosophy should include the study of politics, aesthetics . . . In fact, I think it should be an all-embracing subject. I also think English philosophers ought to take cognizance of Continental thought. I feel uncomfortable talking about philosophy. I don't really like to talk about things when I'm writing about them, and since I write philosophy, I try to avoid it in conversation as much as possible." But he went on to say he hoped that his new book had put him in the middle of the cultural stream of Europe. He said that, like Miss Murdoch, he was very much interested in Existentialism and literature, and, indeed, was now mostly working on aesthetics.

He and Ayer shared many friends, but his closest friend was Isaiah Berlin. He had just spent two weeks with him in Italy. "Isaiah, rather indirectly," he said, "does illustrate one great aspect of Oxford philosophy — the boon of just talking. As you know, he learned most of his philosophy at the feet of Austin. They were both at All Souls at the same time, in the thirties, and they used to sit around in the Common Room and talk philosophy day and night. During the war, once, Isaiah found himself in a plane, without Austin, and some mysterious thing happened that made him decide to give up philosophy." Hampshire thought that Berlin now regretted giving up philosophy, mainly because he missed the intellectual stimulation of talking. He had no one to talk with about his subject — the history of ideas. There were only one or two great historians of ideas, and they were not at Oxford, so Berlin was forced to work in solitude. Since his great conversational gifts could not be exercised in the service of his work, he relied on an occasional American postgraduate student who was studying ideas to bring him out of the isolation ward of his subject. The reason Berlin could not be counted as an Oxford philosopher was simple. He worked not at pure but at political philosophy. Where a pure philosopher might begin by asking the meaning of the word "liberty," Berlin opened one of his lectures by saying, "There are two sorts of notions of the word 'liberty' — negative and positive — in the history of thought. Kant, Fichte, Hegel believed . . ."

Hampshire rose to get another drink and was pounced upon by an African youth of about sixteen who had heard him speak in a public lecture hall. "Sir, do you mind if I join you?" he asked, edging his way over to our table.

"If you really want to," Hampshire said, sounding a little discouraged. He bought the boy a double whiskey and placed it before him.

The boy only sniffed at it, while discomfiting Hampshire with repeated compliments. "I heard, sir," he said, "you're a man of great vision, really very great vision, and you believe in equality — independence for Algerians and Maltese."

Hampshire asked him about his interests, and the boy said that he'd always wanted to be an engineer, but that since hearing Hampshire he had wondered whether he ought not to be a philosopher. "I'm torn in my conscience," he remarked, with a sigh.

Hampshire counselled him to be an engineer. "In that way, you can do more for your country," he said.

After a while, the boy left, but the philosophical calm — if it could be called that — of our conversation had been shattered. Hampshire moved his hands restlessly, and, after some nervous false starts, began reviewing the gallery of Oxford philosophers. His words were reeled off in the rapid fashion of All Souls conversation, and the philosophical lights whizzed past. "On occasion, Wittgenstein would say, 'Wittgenstein, Wittgenstein, Wittgenstein,' the 'W' Anglicized into a soft sound, instead of the Teutonic 'V,' 'you are talking nonsense,' and he would smite his brow. He was the only person permitted — and no doubt the only person qualified — to utter that particular proposition. . . . Among other things, Austin was the chairman of the financial committee of the Oxford University Press — the biggest university press in the world. He occupied the post with an enveloping halo, and his terrifying efficiency raised him above all past and future chairmen. . . . Elizabeth Anscombe, in some ways, is like Wittgenstein — she even has his mannerisms. Her classes, like the Master's, are brooding séances. She wrote a series of letters to the *Listener* in which she opposed awarding former President Truman an honorary degree, because of his responsibility for dropping the atom bomb. She made an extraordinary speech at the concilium, saying, 'If you honor

Truman now, what Neros, what Genghis Khans, what Hitlers, what Stalins will you honor next?' . . . Hare is a little puritanical in his views. . . . Miss Murdoch is elusive. . . . Warnock talks slowly — a thin sheath over his sharp mind for those who've only met him once. . . . Strawson, very exciting. Though sometimes may build a spiral staircase for his thought out of hairsplitting distinctions. . . . Ayer, like Russell, well known as a philosopher, brilliant performer on television, who, among all his other achievements, can simplify. . . . Gellner's charge that these philosophers have things in common will not bear examination. Sociology can be bad history. Sometimes classifies its subjects of study indiscriminately. Gellner may be a victim of his own art. Good with the Berbers."

After saying goodbye to Hampshire, I returned to John's rooms and took from the shelf "Ludwig Wittgenstein: A Memoir," by Norman Malcolm, with a prefatory biographical sketch by Professor Georg Henrik von Wright, of the University of Helsinki. Because each meeting with a philosopher had made me more curious about Wittgenstein, I set myself the task of finding out more about him.

Ludwig Josef Johann Wittgenstein was born in 1889. His parents were Saxon, but at the time of his birth they were living in Vienna. His paternal grandfather was a convert from Judaism to Protestantism; his mother, however, was a Catholic, and the child was baptized in her faith. His father was an engineer, whose remarkable intelligence and will power had raised him to a leading position in the steel-and-iron industry of the Austro-Hungarian Empire. Ludwig was one of eight children. Both of his parents were extremely musical, and their home was a center of artistic activity. He received his early education at home, learning mathematics and the clarinet, and acquiring a burning boyhood wish to become a conductor. At fourteen, he was sent to a school in Linz, and after three years there he was ready for the engineering course at the Technische Hochschule in Berlin. He completed his Berlin course in two years and went to England, where he registered at the University of Manchester as a research student. His first step on the path of philosophy was the reading of Bertrand Russell's "Principles of Mathematics," published in 1903, to which he turned when he wished to plumb the foundations of mathematics. After Russell, he read Gottlob Frege, the German mathematician, thus coming face to face with the two most brilliant exponents of the "new" logic. He sought out Frege in Jena, only to be directed by him to go back to England and study with Russell. By 1912, he was housed in Trinity College, Cambridge, whose walls also enclosed Bertrand Russell, G. E. Moore, and John Maynard Keynes. Young Wittgenstein was immediately befriended by them, and he found himself part of the golden years of Cambridge. He was there for eighteen months, and, in addition to his other work, did some psychological experiments in rhythm and music. Even though he was on intimate terms with the leading minds of England, he did not take to the relaxed atmosphere of Cambridge life. In the autumn of 1913, he visited Norway, and he returned there later that same year in a sort of intellectual huff, to live in seclusion near Skjolden; he soon became fluent in Norwegian. His father had died in 1912, and his stay at Manchester and Cambridge had simply driven him deeper into a depression whose history was as long as his life. "It is probably true that he lived on the border of mental illness," Professor von Wright says at the opening of his sketch. "A fear of being driven across it followed him throughout his life." The outbreak of the First World War found him a volunteer in the Austrian Army, and he eventually fought on both the eastern and southern fronts. For Wittgenstein, war was a time of personal crisis and of the birth of great ideas. At one moment he was calmed by Leo Tolstoy's ethical writings — which led him to the warm light of the Synoptic Gospels — and at the next he was excited by his own revolutionary views.

Wittgenstein's earthquake hit the philosophers of the twentieth century as hard as David Hume's cyclone — which swept away cause and effect from the human experience — had hit their eighteenth-century predecessors. The new philosophical shudder started at the Austrian front. One day in the middle of the war, while Wittgenstein was reading a newspaper in a trench, he was arrested by a sketch of a possible sequence of events in a car accident. As he studied it, he became aware that the diagram of the accident stood for a possible pattern of occurrences in reality; there was a correspondence between the parts of the drawing and certain things in the world. He noticed a similar correspondence between the parts of a sentence and elements of the world, and he developed the analogy, coming to regard a proposition as a kind of picture. The structure of a proposition — that is, the way in which the parts of a statement were combined — depicted a possible combination of elements in reality. Thus he hit upon the central idea of his "Tractatus": Language was the picture of the world. The "Tractatus" and the Wittgenstein revolution in philosophy were under way.

When Wittgenstein was captured by the Italians, in 1918, he had the manuscript of his first great philosophical work in his rucksack, and he was able to bring it through the war intact. He thought his masterpiece had solved all philosophical problems, and when the work was published (first in Germany, in 1921, and then in England, the following year), some leading minds agreed, with him, that philosophy had come to the end of its road. Wittgenstein, on the other hand, was at the beginning of his. Both his livelihood and his reputation were assured. He had inherited a large fortune from his father, his genius was proclaimed to the world, and he was free to live in leisure and intellectual preëminence. But such safe ways were not those of Ludwig Wittgenstein. In the first year after the war, he renounced his fortune, became indifferent to the success of the

"Tractatus," and enrolled in a teachers' college in Vienna. When he had completed his education course, he taught in schools in Lower Austria for six years, wandering from one remote village to another. Being a schoolmaster enabled him to lead a life of simplicity and seclusion, but Wittgenstein was not at peace with himself or the world. He gave up the profession and for a time became a gardener, working mostly at monasteries, and, as he had done in the past, considered joining a religious order. Once more, however, the monastic life did not seem to be the answer. Terminating his restless wanderings, he returned to Vienna, and spent two solid years designing and constructing a mansion for one of his sisters. A modern building of concrete, steel, and glass, it provided an outlet for his particular architectural genius, and according to Professor von Wright, "Its beauty is of the same simple and static kind that belongs to the sentences of the 'Tractatus.'" But architecture could not contain Wittgenstein's soaring genius, and he spent some time sculpturing at a friend's studio. Again according to Professor von Wright, his sculpture of an elf has a perfection of symmetry that recalls the Greeks. Wittgenstein's period of withdrawal from philosophy was now nearing an end. In Vienna, he heard a philosophical lecture and decided that perhaps philosophy did have a little way to go, so he allowed his old friend Keynes to raise some money for his return to Cambridge. He arrived at his college in 1929, and presented his "Tractatus" as a dissertation for a Doctorate of Philosophy — a degree that was a negligible accolade to a philosopher with a worldwide reputation. A year later, at the age of forty-one, he was elected a Fellow of Trinity College, Cambridge.

As suddenly as a sketch of a car accident had inspired the ideas in "Tractatus," so a gesture of an Italian friend destroyed them. The gesture that divided Wittgenstein I from Wittgenstein II was made sometime in the year 1933. "Wittgenstein and P. Sraffa, a lecturer in economics at Cambridge, argued together a great deal over the ideas of the 'Tractatus,'" Professor Malcolm records. "One day (they were riding, I think, on a train), when Wittgenstein was insisting that a proposition and that which it describes must have the same 'logical form,' the same 'logical multiplicity,' Sraffa made a gesture, familiar to Neapolitans as meaning something like disgust or contempt, of brushing the underneath of his chin with an outward sweep of the fingertips of one hand. And he asked: 'What is the logical form of that?' Sraffa's example produced in Wittgenstein the feeling that there was an absurdity in the insistence that a proposition and what it describes must have the same 'form.' This broke the hold on him of the conception that a proposition must literally be a 'picture' of the reality it describes." It was many years before Wittgenstein II worked out his new ideas, but the old views, which at one time had finished philosophy forever, were discarded in the train.

Wittgenstein II, though he spent thirteen years at Cambridge, did not surround himself with any of the atmosphere of an English college. The stark simplicity of his way of living would have put any undergraduate to shame. His two rooms in Whewell's Court were like barracks; he did not have a single book, painting, photograph, or reading lamp. He sat on a wooden chair and did his writing at a card table. These two objects, with two canvas chairs, a fireproof safe for his manuscripts, and a few empty flowerpots, constituted the total furnishings of the room that served him as both study and classroom. His other concession to life was a cot, in the second room.

His classes were held late in the afternoon, and his pupils arrived carrying chairs from the landing. They always found the philosopher standing in the middle of the room, by his wooden chair. He was slender, of medium height, and simply dressed, habitually wearing a flannel shirt, flannel trousers, a leather jacket, and no tie. Unlike the other Fellows, he did not have any notes or set procedure for his lectures; he just sat on his wooden chair and, according to Malcolm, "carried on a visible struggle with his thoughts." His lectures were simply a continuation of his other waking hours; as always, he thought about problems and tried to find new solutions. The principal difference between his lonely hours and the lecture time was the difference between a monologue and a dialogue. He would direct questions to the members of the class and let himself be drawn into discussions, but whenever he sensed that he was standing on the edge of a difficult problem or a new thought, his hand would silence his interlocutor with a peremptory motion. If he reached an impasse or felt confused, he would say, "I'm just too stupid today," or "You have a dreadful teacher," or "I'm a fool." He worried about the possibility that his teaching might stop the growth of independent minds, and he was also besieged by a fear that he would not be able to last the period, but somehow he always managed to go on.

The years of the Second World War found Wittgenstein working as an orderly, first at Guy's Hospital, in London, and then in an infirmary at Newcastle-upon-Tyne. Toward the close of the war, he returned to Cambridge to take up the Chair of Philosophy. When Malcolm returned there to study with him, in 1946, he found Wittgenstein trying, with strenuous work, to dam the depression that always threatened to flood him. Wittgenstein was composing his "Philosophical Investigations" (which he kept on revising for the rest of his life). "One day," Malcolm recounts, "when Wittgenstein was passing a field where a football game was in progress, the thought first struck him that in language we play *games* with *words*. A central idea of his philosophy [in "Investigations"], the notion of a 'language game,' apparently had its genesis in this incident." At this time, most of his day was spent in teaching, talking, and writing the "Investigations." His only relief from the constant motion of his thoughts was an occasional film or an American detective magazine. But this was no opiate, and he ultimately felt compelled to tender his resignation to the Vice-Chancellor of the university. Late in 1947, when the decision was taken, he wrote to Malcolm, "I shall cease to be professor on Dec. 31st at 12 P.M." He did. Now began the loneliest period of his never convivial life. He first moved to a guesthouse a couple of hours' bus ride from Dublin, where he lived friendless and in a state of nervous instability. He tired easily, and his work on "Investigations" went slowly and painfully. He wrote to Malcolm that he did not miss conversation but wished for "someone to smile at occasionally." After five months at the guesthouse, he migrated to the west coast of Ireland, where he became a legend among the primitive fishermen for his power to tame birds. But there was no rest for him. He went to Vienna, visited Cambridge, returned to Dublin, rushed again to Vienna, where a sister was now dangerously ill, proceeded from there to America to see the Malcolms, and was forced back to England and Cambridge by an undiagnosed illness. He was eventually found to have cancer. His father had been destroyed by this disease, and his sister was even then dying of it. He left for Austria and his family, but some months later he returned to England — this time to Oxford, which he quickly came to dislike. He called it "the influenza area" and "a philosophical desert." After spending some time at Miss Anscombe's house in Oxford, he visited Norway, only to return to Cambridge and live with his doctor. Never a happy man, he became convinced during the last two years of his life that he had lost his philosophical talent; he was also haunted by the suicides of three of his brothers. He died in April, 1951.

I read the last paragraph of Malcolm's memoir: "When I think of his profound pessimism, the intensity of his mental and moral suffering, the relentless way in which he drove his intellect, his need for love together with the harshness that repelled love, I am inclined to believe that his life was fiercely unhappy. Yet at the end he himself exclaimed that it had been 'wonderful!' To me this seems a mysterious and strangely moving utterance."

When John returned, he found me in a sombre mood.

"Yes," he said. "Wittgenstein was a tortured genius. He could have been a first-class conductor, mathematician, architect, or sculptor, but he chose to be a philosopher." He started leafing through "A Memoir," and read aloud: "'A person caught in a philosophical confusion is like a man in a room who wants to get out but doesn't know how. He tries the window but it is too high. He tries the chimney but it is too narrow. And if he would only *turn around*, he would see that the door has been open all the time!'"

To both of us, this particular passage seemed to stand as an epitaph for Ludwig Wittgenstein.

Next morning, I rolled out of my makeshift bed and, with the help of my jottings, started writing furiously the conclusions of my researches. To my great surprise, complicated sentences streamed out of my typewriter and I discovered that I had a philosophical voice keyed somehow to the right pitch.

"Modern philosophy," I wrote, "has had two great pushes, one from Russell and one from Wittgenstein, and we're now waiting for another one. Like all philosophies, its claim to be heard rests on two assumptions: first, that what it says is true and lucid; second, that these particular truths are more satisfying than any alternative answers to the inquiring and reflective mind. Naturally, not all reflective minds will be better satisfied at Oxford than, say, in Paris, Moscow, New Delhi, or New York, but some clearly are. Oxford philosophers do not claim to be sages. In few cases, indeed, would the claim be credited if it should be made. By their own admission, they are not wiser than other men. They often assert that their researches do not lead to wisdom but only relieve certain feelings of puzzlement (which you are bound to have if you ask their questions). Once they have found answers to their questions, they go on living just as before, and, unlike their French contemporaries, many remain *dégagé;* they lead dons' comfortable lives in north Oxford (though even so a few manage to be evangelists, Socialists, or great eccentrics). This has led Gellner to ask what the point of their activities can be, since they seem to cure only a disease they have induced in themselves and, in many cases, in their students. Why should one pay philosophers, he asks, if philosophy really, as Wittgenstein said, 'leaves the world as it is'? Gellner's is a mistaken objection. Certainly many philosophers are unadventurous, prosaic, and boring, but there are also Strawsons and Ayers and plenty of others who are not. Whatever they may do in their private lives, it cannot correctly be said that in their work they 'leave the world as it is.' If one man begins to see more clearly how the *rest* of the world is, then the world is not as it was. One man sees more truth than was seen in the past; the more widely this truth is disseminated, the more the world is changed. Indeed, once one considers this, Gellner's criticism seems absurd. For philosophy has never changed the world except by bringing to consciousness in the minds that engage in it certain truths that they did not know (or did not know clearly) before. Oxford philosophers are fond of quoting a remark of Wittgenstein's to the effect that there need be nothing in common among all the members of a class of things called by the same name. If we must generalize about the Oxford philosophers and their subject, their philosophy is essentially agnostic, not in respect to the question of God's existence but in relation to many of the great problems whose definitive solution has in the past been taken as the aim of philosophy: questions like whether life is meaningful, whether history has a purpose, whether human nature is good — in fact, all the questions that have to be asked when a man reflectively considers the question 'How should I live?' It is true that most Oxford philosophers are not agnostic in religion; on the contrary, several are Catholic or Protestant communicants. But they regard these matters as being outside their philosophy. As men, they decide to answer these questions in one way; as philosophers, they teach and develop techniques that are neutral in respect to the different answers to them.

"Oxford philosophers tend to talk chiefly to each other — and, in cases like Wittgenstein's, to themselves. These practitioners are highly technical (even if they claim they make a 'technique of being non-technical'). There are exceptions: Ayer is one; another is Hampshire, who on some subjects — especially literary subjects, as opposed to philosophical ones — succeeds in being illuminating to the simple. Still, most of the philosophers go on thinking that technical philosophy is a good thing, necessary in order to keep the subject from 'popularization,' which they interpret as oversimplification or quackery. The pity is that their insistence on professionalism means that 'ordinary men' are left not without any philosophy at all but with old, dead, or quack varieties of it. Oxford philosophy, by comparison with the past, is non-systematic. Where traditional practitioners thought it right to deal with questions like 'What is Truth?,' Oxford philosophers are liable to say, following the later Wittgenstein, 'Look at all the different ways the word "true" is used in ordinary speech.' (They refuse to look into the uses of words in extraordinary speech, like poetry, because English philosophy has been dominated since Hume by a prosaic contempt for the imagination.) When you have considered all the ways 'true' is used in ordinary speech, they say, you have understood the concept of 'Truth.' If there is a further question lingering at the back of your mind ('But all the same, what *is* Truth?'), this is the result of a mistake — a hangover from reading earlier philosophers. This approach — philosophy as the study of language rather than as the means of answering the big questions about life and the universe — which is basically that of the later Wittgenstein, has given Oxford philosophy a tendency to formlessness. Until recently, the body of philosophical thought has existed mainly in a vast number of small articles minutely considering a few uses of some single concept. Only the aesthetic sense of some of its practitioners — Wittgenstein I, Ayer, Hampshire, Strawson, and a few others — has kept it from overwhelming diffuseness.

"Now there is a change coming. The Oxford school is breaking up; all the signs are that there isn't going to be an orthodoxy much longer — that things are going to get eccentric again. Austin is no more, and at the moment Ryle is not producing. Strawson is going in for talking about metaphysics in the old vein, and there is every indication that the Wittgenstein wave is petering out rather rapidly. In the ten years since Ryle tried to solve the mind-body problem by a vast number of small chapters on different psychological concepts in 'The Concept of Mind,' Oxford philosophy has begun to develop its own system builders. Probably the strict discipline of the late Austin helped induce guilt about the looseness and untidiness that these uncoördinated researches — each one precise and tidy — were creating in the subject as a whole. Two recent books, Hampshire's 'Thought and Action' and Strawson's 'Individuals,' offer quite systematic approaches to some of the most puzzling traditional problems in philosophy: the value of freedom of thought and the relation of intelligence to morality, in the first; the problem of sense data and the mind-body puzzle, in the second. The new systematic quality comes from a recent insight: that while linguistic philosophy is the study of language, certain wider truths *can* be deduced from the conditions that must be presupposed if there is to be language at all — or language of the kind we have. On propositions deduced from the statement of such conditions, necessary truths (like the relation between the mind and the body) can be built systematically. The non-systematic decades may have been an aberration — partly, no doubt, owing to the tendency of philosophers to imitate Wittgenstein II and his stylistic lapses from the poetic and architectural sensibility he displayed in the 'Tractatus.' As Shakespeare said of the pedants in 'Love's Labour's Lost,' 'They have been at a great feast of languages, and stolen the scraps. O! they have lived long on the alms-basket of words.' But then, as the proverb, more than two thousand years old, has it, 'Those that study particular sciences and neglect philosophy'— however defined and however studied —'are like Penelope's wooers, who made love to the waiting-women.'"

These sentences were no sooner out of my typewriter than they seemed to have been written by a stranger. Reading them over, I couldn't shake loose the feeling that they were one more walker on that common street where on a morning stroll I'd first met Lord Russell.

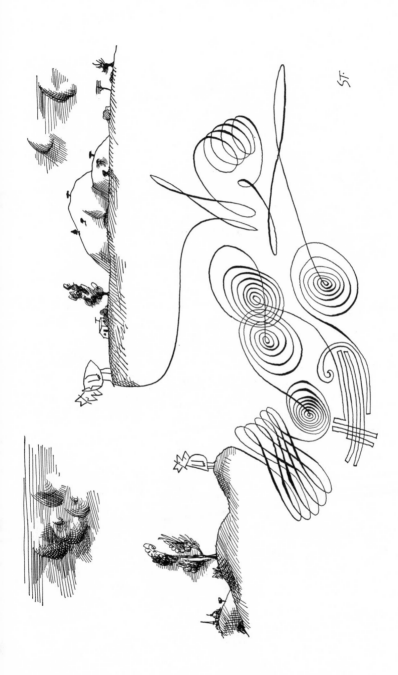

Argument Without End

In the course of my philosophical conversation with Russell, he had remarked, sucking his pipe, "When I was an undergraduate, there were many boys cleverer than I, but I surpassed them, because, while they were *dégagé*, I had passion and fed on controversy. I still thrive on opposition. My grandmother was a woman of caustic and biting wit. When she was eighty-three, she became kind and gentle. I had never found her so reasonable. She noticed the change in herself, and, reading the handwriting on the wall, she said to me, 'Bertie, I'll soon be dead.' And she soon was." Since Earl Russell was well up in his eighties at the time of this talk, I calculated that he must have spent nearly seventy adult years in devoted altercation. Whatever progress the stragglers on the easy road of cleverness might have made, there was no doubt that the tough, intrepid Russell had reached success by clambering up the brambly and precipitous path of intellectual controversy. Russell's words pandered to my long-standing predilection for following intellectual escapades, with the aid of newspaper dispatches, from the ease of my armchair. Since one of the subjects I am particularly interested in happens to be history — I read it at Oxford — the thorny journeys that have stood out most sharply in the newssheets have concerned historians. The parties have more often than not been made up of Englishmen, and their terrain has been Britain. The smallness of English intellectual society, the availability of space in newspapers and periodicals of the better class (indeed, their encouragement of controversial material), the highly individual and belligerent nature of English scholars — all have made England the perfect country for such energetic pursuits. Nor was my choice of history — a subject known for its uncertainties, revisions, and tentative truths — a bad one; it appeared to be fair game all the way.

My safari in search of historical truth didn't exactly have a beginning, but the *Encounter* article entitled "Arnold Toynbee's Millennium" (June, 1957), by H. R. Trevor-Roper — who was appointed Regius Professor of Modern History at Oxford in 1957 — was a memorable blast that could easily have set me off. The ten-volume "A Study of History," which Trevor-Roper was ostensibly reviewing, was the product of more than twenty years' labor by one of the most tireless and single-minded men of our time, Arnold Joseph Toynbee, Professor Emeritus of the University of London and former Director of Studies at the Royal Institute of International Affairs, London. With unflagging zeal he had examined the history of six thousand years — the life cycles of a score of civilizations. He concluded that civilizations spring from a response to challenges, and that they flourish by the power of a "creative minority," and that they collapse with its failure, secreting sometimes amid the ruins a religion and a new society. Charting the series of challenges that produced great responses and higher religions, as well as those that did not, he thought he had proved that religions and creative minorities make civilizations and that the dead weight of majorities and schisms unmakes them. Of all the societies considered, Western civilization alone, for Toynbee, still lives, and even it has been tottering since the Reformation. Its chances of redemption were faced in the last four volumes. There it appeared that the weight of historical laws is against our survival, but Toynbee insisted, rather contradictorily, that man is blessed with free will and that history cannot rob him of it. Our Western civilization can be saved by a recourse to faith, syncretist variety.

Both the commercial success of the "Study" ("As a dollar-earner . . . it ranks second only to whiskey," Trevor-Roper gibed) and the despair that flowed from the latter volumes galled Trevor-Roper. As was noted at the time, the personal venom that shot out of Trevor-Roper's pen had seldom, if ever, been equalled in the writings of modern scholarship. (In 1957, Trevor-Roper was generally known for one youthful work on a seventeenth-century archbishop, which was distinctive for being anticlerical, and for a brilliant but rather journalistic account of the last days of Hitler; but particularly among scholars for some powerful attacks on his academic brethren in periodicals, notably R. H. Tawney, who was acknowledged to be one of the great English historians, and Lawrence Stone, of Wadham College, Oxford, whom Trevor-Roper wounded at the start of Stone's teaching career.) Now he bellowed that, compared with Toynbee's style, the writings of Hitler had a "Gibbonian lucidity," and declared that the "Study" was "huge, presumptuous, and utterly humourless," and not only "erroneous" but "hateful." He wrote, "Toynbee's truly monstrous self-adulation combined with his fundamental obscurantism [does] indeed emotionally repel me." For the *Encounter* critic, the "Study" was an extravagant bid of Toynbee to set himself up as a prophet — a Hitler. Had not "Hitler, like . . . Toynbee . . . ranged over the centuries and crammed such facts as he found it convenient to select into a monstrous system"? Did not both Hitler and Toynbee see themselves as the phoenixes of the centuries, Messiahs who had rolled up Western civilization and opened up a new age — in Hitler's case the Nazi era, and in Toynbee's the wishful age of a syncretist religion of all faiths, "a new *tutti-frutti* . . . 'a mish-mash,' as one commentator has described it, 'of the Virgin Mary and Mother Isis, of St. Michael and Mithras, of St. Peter and

Mohammed, of St. Augustine and Jalalad-Din Maw-lana'"? To Trevor-Roper, the scheming Messiah had given himself away at the beginning and the end of the tenth volume — in the acknowledgments, where he expressed his gratitude to, in Trevor-Roper's words, "all who, since the beginning of History, have deserved immortality by contributing . . . to that ultimate creation of the ages, the mind of Toynbee," and in the index, where Trevor-Roper, by diligent use of the tape measure, discovered that the entry "Toynbee, Arnold Joseph" occupied twelve column inches. With an ardor somewhat in excess of many hounding reviewers, Trevor-Roper transported himself to the centenary of the birth of the Messiah ("A.T. 100") and found the devotees faithfully reading the Old Testament (the six prewar volumes) and the New Testament (the four postwar volumes). In all the churches of Mish-Mash, they were reciting "the drowsy doggerel of the Founder's Litany 'Mother Mary, Mother Isis, Mother Cybele, Mother Ishtar, Mother Kwanyin, have compassion on us. . . .'" No spirit of fun, however, was at work in the review. ("Am I serious? Alas, I am," the writer noted with chilling humor.) Indeed, the attack was so grave that it created a minor sensation, especially since it coincided with talk of Trevor-Roper's appointment to the Regius Chair of Modern History at Oxford, one of the most coveted academic gifts of Her Majesty's Government. Many, including quite a few Oxford students — and they often don't like Toynbee any more than does

Trevor-Roper — seemed to be as repelled by Trevor-Roper's attack as he was by Toynbee's work, and when the appointment was made, some months later, they questioned its advisability. They were supported in their doubts by the London *Observer,* which noted that some people were "wondering about the influence on under-graduates of a man capable of writing a considered article with such elaborate violence and personal hatred."

For some time, there wasn't the faintest whisper of a reply from Toynbee; two final volumes of the "Study" were delivered as though Trevor-Roper had never written. Debate, controversy, the arrows of cleverdom were not weapons in Toynbee's quiver. Then, after many years of silence, he did try to answer all his critics in a heavy volume called "Reconsiderations," but the book was remarkable for the absence of any bite. Trevor-Roper, the cruelest and most lacerating critic, was barely acknowledged. Out of seven references to him, four were in the footnotes, and only one betrayed a hint of exasperation. ("On the article as a whole, no comment," Toynbee said, with a rare shrug.) Was Toynbee a prophet, as Trevor-Roper had charged? "The imputation," Toynbee noted, with exaggerated courtesy, "is difficult to deal with, because the next most ridiculous thing to saying, 'I think I am a prophet' would be to say, 'I really don't think I am.' Perhaps the best answer is not a verbal but a practical one. A readiness to believe that one may have been mistaken in the views that one has expressed is surely incompatible with believing that they are not one's own, but God's. So I hope this volume of reconsiderations may effectively dissipate the spectre of 'Toynbee the prophet.'"

During the first years of Trevor-Roper's professorship, there was an uneasy lull in his activities. Some said that the professorship had mellowed him, others that he was crouching in wait for big shikar. Everybody was guessing, some people with a greater degree of apprehension than others, but Sir Harold Nicolson, *doyen* of critics, appeared able to tread on Trevor-Roper's toes with impunity. Writing of the only book issued ex cathedra — a collection of the Professor's miscellaneous reviews — Nicolson commented, "It seems to me that the Professor, for all the fine finality of his judgments, lacks the daring scope of Toynbee, the majesty of Namier, the incisive wit of A. J. P. Taylor, the taste of Miss Wedgwood, the humanity of Trevelyan, or the charm and modesty of Dr. A. L. Rowse. . . . Among the strings of his lute there is a wire of hate which is apt to twang suddenly with the rasp of a banjo." Nevertheless, it was believed that if there was a case to be stated against a historian, Trevor-Roper could marshal and present the evidence not only more destructively but more elegantly than anyone else.

It was after nearly five years of the professorship that a very spectacular fatted calf presented himself; he was A. J. P. Taylor, Fellow of Magdalen College, Oxford. Unlike Toynbee, Taylor looked for no grand design or purpose in the universe, claimed no theory of history.

He was a polyglot scholar who had written about a dozen historical studies, many of which were standard works in his chosen period of the nineteenth and twentieth centuries. If anything, he was more illustrious prey than Toynbee; while practically everybody had stalked Toynbee, not many had dared to pursue Taylor. In the eyes of the professionals, Taylor had as many solid books to his name as any living historian. True, many of them held against Taylor his regular contributions to certain sections of the vulgar press, like the *Sunday Express* (the fact that he wrote just as often for highbrow papers did not seem to redeem him), and his regular television appearances — his *Who's Who* entry boasts, "Appears regularly in television programme, Free Speech," and lists among his publications, " 'The Russian Revolution of 1917' . . . (script of first lectures ever given on television)"— but since a journalistic don was not a very uncommon phenomenon in England, Taylor got away with all this, and more, until Trevor-Roper came along, in yet another *Encounter* article —"A. J. P. Taylor, Hitler, and the War" (July, 1961) — to slaughter him. The book under attack this time was Taylor's "The Origins of the Second World War." It had arrived on the historical scene like a thunderbolt, unheralded by the usual prepublication talk. While the specialists retired to their dens to chew over the "Origins," Taylor's book, like Toynbee's work before it, received handsome encomiums from the public at large. The *New Statesman* review, for one, began, "Mr. A. J. P. Taylor is the only English historian now writing who can bend the bow of Gibbon and Macaulay." It went on to claim that the book was "a masterpiece: lucid, compassionate, beautifully written in a bare, sparse style, and at the same time deeply disturbing." It was disturbing because Taylor assailed the assumption that Hitler and his henchmen had willed the war. He termed this universally held belief a myth, and concluded, in one disquieting sentence, "The war of 1939, far from being premeditated, was a mistake, the result on both sides of diplomatic blunders." The historian depicted Hitler as a rational and serious statesman whose foreign policy had a long pedigree. The implications of this view were far-reaching. To take one instance — as book reviewers noted — if Hitler was not a madman, then all Germans were guilty.

Trevor-Roper soon emerged from his library, and his article on Taylor was only a little less violent than his response to Toynbee. In the "Study," the prophecy had repelled him; what repelled him in the "Origins" seemed to be the philosophy —though Taylor was no more ready to admit he was a philosopher than Toynbee had been to admit that he was a prophet. In fact, Taylor insisted that he was simply trying "to tell the story as it may appear to some future historian, working from the records." The philosophy that Trevor-Roper ascribed to Taylor would scarcely fill a paragraph in any philosopher's notebook. According to Trevor-Roper, Taylor thought that there were no heroes or villains in history, and that "the real determinants of history . . . are objective situations and human blunders." According to Taylor, Trevor-Roper continued, "objective situations consist of the realities of power; human intelligence is best employed in recognizing these realities and allowing events to conform with them; but as human intelligence seldom prevails in politics, the realities generally have to assert themselves, at greater human cost through the mess caused by human blunders." Taylor might claim to be writing from the records, Trevor-Roper said, but his philosophy could write his history for him. This was how, in Trevor-Roper's view, both Hitler and Neville Chamberlain could be painted by Taylor as "intelligent statesmen": Both, it seemed, followed the "historical necessity" of 1918. Since Germany was not carved up after its defeat, it tended to revert to its natural position of a great power. Hitler was, therefore, right and intelligent in coöperating with this "historical necessity," for he stood to gain, and Chamberlain was also intelligent in yielding to the same "historical necessity," though he stood to lose. With such a philosophy, how could there be heroes or villains? Trevor-Roper's insinuation was that any historian who looked at the world with these neutral eyes obviously could not see the true Adolf Hitler.

If a historian was unable to see Hitler, whose life was within our memory — what could he see, I wondered. The charge was all the more severe for being applied to a long-established and brilliant practitioner of the historical art. And how had Taylor come to such a pass? Trevor-Roper had his theories. He exhumed an old controversy about the Regius Chair. The late Sir Lewis Namier, accepted by Toynbee, Taylor, and Trevor-Roper himself as a historian without equal in twentieth-century England, had, it was publicly rumored, recommended Trevor-Roper over his pupil, Taylor, for the Regius Chair, on the ground that Trevor-Roper was a preferable academic candidate for not having appeared much on television. "Is it, as some have suggested," Trevor-Roper now asked in *Encounter,* "a gesture of posthumous defiance to his former master, Sir Lewis Namier, in revenge for some imagined slight? If so, it is just as well that it is posthumous: otherwise what devastating justice it·would have received!" His speculations on Taylor's motives did not stop here. He went on, "Is it, as Mr. Taylor's friends prefer to believe, mere characteristic *gaminerie,* the love of firing squibs and laying banana-skins to disconcert the gravity and upset the balance of the orthodox? Or does Mr. Taylor perhaps suppose that such a re-interpretation of the past will enable us better to face the problems of the present? Theoretically, this should not be his motive, for not only does Mr. Taylor, in his book, frequently tell us that the past has never pointed the course of the future, but he has also assured us recently, in the *Sunday Express,* that the study of history can teach nothing, not even general understanding: its sole purpose, he says, is to amuse; and it would therefore seem to have no more right to a place in education than the blowing of soap bubbles or other forms of innocent recreation." I wondered if the historian who made soap bubbles out of history would answer or retreat behind the dignified cloak of silence, as Toynbee had done a few years earlier. A day or two later, this question was settled for me, apparently, when I received the June 9th copy of the *Times Literary Supplement.* In a disturbing letter of two sentences, Taylor dismissed the host of learned critics who, like Trevor-Roper, had been dogging him and a kind *T.L.S.* reviewer. "I have no sympathy with authors who resent criticism or try to answer it," he wrote. "I must however thank your correspondents for the free publicity which they have given my book."

Nevertheless, I looked through the subsequent *Encounters* for a shriek of protest from Taylor. It took some months in coming, but it was unmistakably there in the September issue, and what a curious form it took! It was ominously headed "HOW TO QUOTE — Exercises for Beginners." Two columns of passages — one from Trevor-Roper's article summarizing and quoting "Origins," and the other unedited quotations from the book — were juxtaposed:

But what about the European Jews? That episode is conveniently forgotten by Mr. Taylor.	Many Germans had qualms as one act of persecution followed another culminating in the unspeakable wickedness of the gaschambers. But few knew

how to protest. Everything which Hitler did against the Jews followed logically from the racial doctrines in which most Germans vaguely believed.

It does not fit the character of a German statesman who "in principle and doctrine, was no more wicked and unscrupulous than many other statesmen."	In principle and doctrine Hitler was no more wicked and unscrupulous than many other contemporary statesmen. In wicked acts he outdid them all.

And so on. But if this was the non-answering way of replying to Trevor-Roper, at the end of his exercise Taylor attempted a variation on the method:

It [the book] will do harm, perhaps irreparable harm, to Mr. Taylor's reputation as a serious historian.	The Regius Professor's methods of quotation might also do harm to his reputation as a serious historian, if he had one.

Appended to Taylor's columns was more prose from Trevor-Roper. This time, his words were defensive, even tame. He wrote that the exercises "are calculated to spare him [Taylor] the trouble of argument and to give a lot of trouble (or, more likely, bewilderment) to the reader," and that "if Mr. Taylor had been able to convict me of any 'quotation' comparable with his own version of the German documents (a subject on which he is now silent), or if he had shown my summary to be as inconsistent with his thesis as he so often is with himself . . . I should indeed be ashamed."

Not long after this, a letter from John, enclosing the transcription of a television confrontation between Trevor-Roper and Taylor on "The Origins of the Second World War," reached me in America. "What a shame you weren't here for the sensational screen struggle," John's epistle read, in part. "Trevor-Roper gave me the impression of spluttering flame under the withering impact of Taylor's mind. Taylor would pinch his nose and take off his glasses as though he had an ulcer or was in pain, and my heart went out to him, while Trevor-Roper appeared nervous, his mouth a little jumpy, his hands writhing. As far as I am concerned, Taylor stole the show. *But this is one man's opinion.* No doubt there are others."

The debate had taken place sometime between the publication of "A. J. P. Taylor, Hitler, and the War" and that of the "Exercises for Beginners." It indicated to me that Taylor certainly hadn't gone down without a fight. While the detailed criticisms of his book had been many and varied, the two points that had drawn everybody's fire were that Taylor was blind to Hitler's wickedness (even if he excluded from the book the genocide of the Jews, on the ground that it was not part of the story of the origins of the war, everybody said, he had no excuse for discounting or ignoring altogether Hitler's monomaniacal visions in "Mein Kampf," his maunderings about being the master of the world in "Hitler's Table Talk, 1941-1944," and his Hossbach Memorandum to the Generals in 1937, which became "the blueprint for the War of 1939") and that Taylor had set out to be perverse (Munich, generally accepted to be "a triumph of cowardice," was made by him "a triumph of all that was best and most enlightened in British life"). In a word, his critics accused him of being an apologist for Hitler, and an apologist for appeasement.

"It's perfectly obvious," Taylor now said in his own defense on TV, "that the wickedness he [Hitler] did, the wickedness he inspired, particularly what went on in Germany — the dictatorship, later on, the extermination of the Jews — these have no parallel in history. I don't dispute this. But it seems to me that his foreign policy was the least original part of what he contributed, either for good or ill. That in this — and this is all I've been trying to say, not thinking of it in moral terms — that Hitler's policy sprang out of the German history that had gone before. That in one form or another Germany, remaining united at the end of the First World War, was bound to seek to destroy the defeat; was bound to seek to undo the Treaty of Versailles; and that the impetus of success in undoing this Treaty would carry Germany forward, unless it was checked in some way, into being again a great and dominant power in Europe. If these are wicked things — if it's wicked for Germans to want to be dominant in Europe, and not wicked, shall

we say, for Americans or Russians to be dominant in the
world, well then he was a wicked statesman. But I don't
understand, except that I dislike the Germans, why
merely wanting your country to be the most powerful
in the world puts you into the head [sic] of a wicked
statesman. . . . The basis of this blueprint [the Hossbach Memorandum] — Hitler lays it down — is that
there's going to be a great war in 1943-45 — he uses these
figures more than once, this is the thing that he's thinking
of, the Great War — which maybe he was planning for
1943-45, instead of that he got himself into a smaller
war in 1939, and how the first can be a blueprint for the
second, I don't understand. If a man comes along, you
know, and says I'm proposing to fly by jet plane to
Canada next year, but instead goes on a motorcycle tour
next week, I don't think he's a very good planner. . . .
The war of 1939 is not the war he planned. It may
well be that he planned some different war — a war
against Russia, a war in 1943, but the war of 1939 was
a war against England and France, it took place against
antagonists that he'd not planned it to take place against,
and it took place at a time when he had not planned
it to take place. . . . When I judge — perhaps this is the
wrong way for a historian to go on — but when I judge
events in the past I try to judge them in terms of the
morality which then existed, not of mine. When I say
that Munich was a triumph for all that was best in
British life, I mean that the years and years before that,
enlightened people, men of the Left — whom perhaps

I equate too easily with all that was best — that they had attacked Czechoslovakia, that they had said that the inclusion of the Sudeten Germans in Czechoslovakia was — in the words of one of them, Brailsford — the worst crime of the peace settlement of 1919. . . . I mean by that a triumph for all those who had preached enlightenment, international conciliation, revision of treaties, the liberation of nationalities from foreign rule, and so on."

For me, the books of Toynbee and Taylor had raised disconcerting questions, which could no longer be answered by arguments over such specific points as whether Toynbee really wished to put out the lights of Western civilization, and whether Taylor overlooked the ferocious and destructive springs of Hitler's character. More fundamental questions had begun to nag at me. The majestic Sir Lewis Namier had furnished his "The Structure of Politics at the Accession of George III" — one of the best historical works of our time — with an epigraph from Aeschylus' "Prometheus Vinctus": "I took pains to determine the flight of crook-taloned birds, marking which were of the right by nature, and which of the left, and what were their ways of living, each after his kind, and the enmities and affections that were between them, and how they consorted together." If, in a sense, history was a movement of birds, Toynbee and Taylor used very different methods to divine it. Both insisted that they were empirical historians, yet one used a telescope and the other a microscope. Both claimed to be objective historians, yet one indisputably tilted his telescope to the heavens and the other, by his own admission, confined the range of his vision to the minutiae of foreign policy. From my study of history, I knew that selection and exclusion were basic principles of the historical method. But the disparity in the procedure of Trevor-Roper's two kills was so great that for me it could not be explained on the grounds of method or temperamental differences. My perplexity, as I was soon to learn, was shared by a Taylor of Cambridge — E. H. Carr, Fellow of Trinity College — who, even as Trevor-Roper was laying low his victims one by one, was asking the question "What is history?" On its own merits, the question was an engulfing one, and the fact that the answers were delivered as Trevelyan lectures to Cambridge undergraduates, broadcast over the B.B.C., reproduced in *Listener* articles, and finally issued as a book, "What Is History?," contributed to the swell of interest.

Carr, one of the most distinguished historians at Cambridge, began his lectures by assailing a few victims of his own with a cutting polemical style that was all the more brilliant and effective for having an air of cogency, reasonableness, and sanity. Prominent in the display of his trophies seemed to be the head of Sir Isaiah Berlin, whose book "The Hedgehog and the Fox" and whose lecture "Historical Inevitability" had established him as a sober and intelligent thinker on the question "What is history?" "In 1954," Carr now said in attacking the Chichele Professor, "Sir Isaiah Berlin published his essay on 'Historical Inevitability.' . . . He added to the indictment the argument . . . that the 'historicism' of Hegel and Marx is objectionable because, by explaining human actions in causal terms, it implies a denial of human free will, and encourages historians to evade their supposed obligation . . . to pronounce moral condemnation on the Charlemagnes, Napoleons, and Stalins of history. . . . Even when he talks nonsense, he earns our indulgence by talking it in an engaging and attractive way."

At the very first opportunity — that is, when Carr's lectures were printed in the spring of 1961, in the *Listener* — Berlin tried to fend Carr off in a letter that finished, "His short way with the problem of individual freedom and responsibility (the 'dead horse' which, in Mr. Carr's horrifying metaphor . . . I 'have flogged into life') is a warning to us all of what may happen to those who, no matter how learned or perspicacious, venture into regions too distant from their own. Mr. Carr speaks of his indulgence towards my follies. I am glad to reciprocate by offering him my sympathy as he gropes his way in the difficult, treacherous and unfamiliar field of philosophy of history."

Carr, however, took Berlin's letter simply as an opportunity to redeliver his thrusts, in the *Listener*, at his new-found sympathizer. He quoted chapter and verse for his summary of Berlin's views:

One [he recited abacus fashion], in "Historical Inevitability" . . . Sir Isaiah writes: "I do not *here* ["my italics," Carr
noted] wish to say that determinism is necessarily false, only
that we neither think nor speak as if it were true and that it
is difficult, and perhaps impossible, to conceive what our picture of the world would be if we seriously believed it." Over
and over again, he seeks to show that determinism is incompatible with "the notion of individual responsibility," . . .
which he emphatically endorses. If these arguments do not
lead to the conclusion that "determinism must be false,"
I do not see where they lead.

Two, Sir Isaiah dismisses what he calls "the modern plea
for a greater effort at understanding" . . . on the ground
that those who make this plea are involved in the fallacy that
"to explain is to understand and to understand is to justify."
This seemed to me to mean that the historian should not look
for, say, underlying social or economic causes of the two
world wars, lest he should in the process explain away the
moral responsibility of Wilhelm II or Hitler or the German
people.

Three, Sir Isaiah sharply dissents from the view . . . "that
it is foolish to judge Charlemagne or Napoleon or Genghis
Khan or Hitler or Stalin for their massacres" and from the
view that it is "absurd" or "not our business as historians" to
praise "benefactors of humanity." I took this to mean that it
is wise and sensible and our business as historians to award
good or bad marks to outstanding figures of the past. . . .

When I wrote my lectures, I thought I knew where he
stood on these three questions. Now, with the best will in the
world, I simply do not know.

To what extent Hitler could help being Hitler, to
what extent he would be morally exonerated if he was
regarded as the product of his environment, to what

extent a historian could place himself in the role of judge — all were more than clockwork hares, even if the scent had stuck to Berlin, who now thumped Carr with a second solid epistle:

(1) My reason for not asserting that determinism must be false is simple — I did not, and do not, know whether it is false. The word "here," italicized by Mr. Carr, was meant to indicate that I did not think it appropriate to conduct a full-scale discussion of the arguments for and against determinism in general in a lecture on history, not (as he seems to think) that I claimed to know it to be false but did not bother to show this in the lecture in question. What I did say, and still believe, is that the arguments in favour of determinism are not convincing, let alone conclusive, and that acceptance of it logically entails a far more drastic revision of some of our commonest convictions and notions than is usually allowed for. The belief, for instance, that men who acted in a particular way in a particular situation could, within certain limits, have acted differently in this same situation, in a more than merely logical sense of "could," seems to me to be one of these.

I argued in my lecture that this assumption underlay the normal thought and language of most men and most historians (including Mr. Carr), whereas they do not imply ability [sic] in determinism as described by Mr. Carr, but rather the contrary. But this fact, although it may create a presumption against determinism, is not, of course, tantamount to showing that determinism is false, still less that it must necessarily be so; only that if it is, at any rate for practical purposes, a valid hypothesis (as it may be), then much that historians and common men (including Mr. Carr) assume or believe will turn out to be false.

I also argued that we cannot really embrace determinism,

that is, incorporate it in our thought and action, without far more revolutionary changes in our language and outlook (some among them scarcely imaginable in terms of our ordinary words and ideas) than are dreamt of in Mr. Carr's philosophy. On the other hand, Mr. Carr is perfectly right in supposing that I believe that the determinist proposition that individual (or indeed any) actions are wholly determined by identifiable causes in time is not compatible with belief in individual responsibility. Mr. Carr believes that both these irreconcilable positions are supported by "common sense and common experience," whereas I think that only the second is what ordinary men assume. It is this paradox that is at the heart of the problem of free-will, and, as I have admitted already, I do not know what its solution is. It is this issue that Mr. Carr dismisses as a "dead horse," as many eminent thinkers have tried to do before him. It has, unfortunately, survived them all and may, I fear, survive him too.

(2) If Mr. Carr supposes that I deny the proposition that "to understand all is to pardon all" he is, once again, perfectly right. But if he infers from this that historians should not, in my view, use all their powers to understand and explain human action, then he is certainly wrong. It seems to me, to give an example, that the better we understand ourselves, the less liable we may be to forgive ourselves for our own actions. But from this it does not begin to follow that historians should not look for "social or economic causes of the two world wars" because their discoveries may explain away the moral responsibility of specific individuals; they may or may not. It is the business of historians to understand and to explain; they are mistaken only if they think that to explain is *ipso facto* to justify or to explain away. This truism would not need stating were it not for a tendency on the part of some modern historians, in their understandable reaction against shallow, arrogant, or philistine moral judgments (and

ignorance or neglect of social and economic causes), to commit themselves to the opposite extreme — the total exoneration of all the actors of history as products of impersonal forces beyond conscious human control.

(3) It is one thing to recognize the right of historians to use words which have moral force, and another to order or recommend historians to deliver moral judgments. I can only say again that to attempt to purge the historian's language of all evaluative force is neither desirable nor possible. But it is a far cry from this to inviting or commanding historians to give marks "to outstanding figures of the past," of which I am accused. In matters of moral judgment historians seem to me to have the same rights and duties, to face the same difficulties, and to be liable to the same lapses as other writers and other men who seek to tell the truth. . . . I sincerely hope, therefore, that in his forthcoming book, which I shall read, like all his other works, with eager interest, he will not charge me with views which neither of us holds. I know that he would not do so willingly.

If Carr had failed to decipher the philosophically coded signals of "Historical Inevitability," he could hardly have failed to understand the letter. But the Cambridge historian unapologetically presented Berlin's head as a trophy in the published book, alongside countless dead and living historians, including Trevor-Roper, who was pinned to the wall as a violent, almost irrational conservative by his own remark "When radicals scream that victory is indubitably theirs, sensible conservatives knock them on the nose." Karl Popper, Professor of Logic and Scientific Method at the London School of Economics, whose "The Open Society and

Its Enemies" had made him a pundit without equal on the philosophy of history, and had also put him at least partly on the side of Carr, was another of Carr's trophies — and that despite the prepublication warnings of E. H. Gombrich, a strong ally of Popper's, who often does his public letter writing. "There is something disarming," Gombrich had noted (again in the *Listener's* epistolary tournament), "in Mr. E. H. Carr's picture of himself as another Galilei, facing a bench of such obscurantist inquisitors as Sir Lewis Namier or Professor Popper . . . while boldly holding on to his Marxist belief in the predetermined movement of history towards ever-increasing human self-awareness. Unfortunately, he is more like Galilei's famous colleague who refused to look through a telescope."

In his book, Carr unhesitatingly held on to his belief, Marxist or no, that all history is relative to the historians who write it, and all historians are relative to their historical and social background. ("Before you study the history, study the historian. . . . Before you study the historian, study his historical and social environment.") History was not objective (possessing a hard core of facts) but subjective (possessing a hard core of interpretation). Each generation reinterpreted history to suit itself, and a good historian was one who projected his vision into the future — or, rather, one whose vision coincided with the goals toward which history was advancing. History was progress, the forward march of events, and a historian was judged to be good if he left the losers on the "rubbish heap of history" and picked the winners of tomorrow. This, as Berlin, who was thus far Carr's severest critic, pointed out, in his final estimation of the book (*New Statesman*), was a "Big Battalion view of history" — although he acclaimed the book as "clear, sharp, excellently written . . . a bold excursion into a region of central importance where most contemporary philosophers and historians, unaccountably, either fear or disdain to tread." Even as I put down Berlin's review, which was remarkable for pulling its punches, rumors reached me that Trevor-Roper, whose conservative views were destined by Carr to join the rubbish heap of history, was bringing out his *Encounter* chopping block.

By this time, my armchair inquiry had grown to compelling proportions, and I was a captive of the delicate art of the philosophy of history. I felt an impulse to talk to the controversialists themselves. After spending a few days in the public library, I came to realize that England is now the home of historians doing historical philosophy, having grasped the leadership from the Germans, who, from Hegel to Oswald Spengler, were unchallenged champions of the subject; today the Continentals who have thoughts on the study tend to gravitate to Britain. I set myself the assignment of finding out what the practicing historians think about their own craft, and what they think the connection is between their craft and their theories of history — hoping at the same time that I would come to know them both as thinkers and as men. Through my reading of history,

I was familiar with the names and writings of many historians who represent various ways of looking at history. Besides Trevor-Roper and Toynbee, Taylor and Carr, there were Herbert Butterfield, Master of Peterhouse, Cambridge; Pieter Geyl, Emeritus Professor of Modern History at the University of Utrecht; C. V. (Veronica) Wedgwood, a scholarly historian who wrote popular history at its best; and a number of others — such quiet English historians as Christopher Hill, Professor R. W. Southern, the Reverend Dr. David Knowles, G. R. Elton, Sir John Neale, David Ogg, and the late Professors Richard Pares and Sir Lewis Namier, who cultivated their scholarly gardens in private. (Berlin and Popper occupy some undefined region between history and philosophy, and their views merit a study by themselves.) With an open list of historians to meet, I started out for the colony of intellectuals, my first stop being the study of Trevor-Roper himself, in the History Faculty Library, on Merton Street, in Oxford.

I found Trevor-Roper — who was born in 1914, the year the First World War started — in his study. He was seated behind a desk in a cold, gray, almost bare room, and he was a youthful-looking gentleman who, one would guess, used a straight razor for a shave. His voice was as bleak as the winter wind from the open window beside his desk, and he had no time for pleasantries. My first few questions fell flat, but mention of the name Taylor made him sit up, rather as a sullen country squire might when he is asked to talk about his grouse shooting.

"I believe in clarity," he said, with a pure B.B.C. accent. "In my article on Taylor, there was not a single emotive word — well, maybe one or two! 'Emotive word' I define as any word that carries with it a value judgment."

I felt I was in the lion's den, but I asked him if speculating on Taylor's motives was not making some sort of value judgment.

"I was following Taylor's stricture in the 'Origins' that one must question the motive of every document," he replied. "For me, Taylor's book is a document, albeit a worthless one. It must, therefore, have a motive. Before speculating on his motives in writing the book, I did consult one or two people — they shall remain nameless."

How did he think the television debate had gone?

"He called me Hughie, but I was not disconcerted or deflected from my manners," he said. "I called him Taylor — though in private life he is known to me as Alan — because I believe that in public debate one must not give the impression of a private coterie. I do not think I did badly."

Had he looked at Toynbee's "Reconsiderations"?

"I refuse to read any of him now," he said. "He is utterly repellent to me. His laws are false. He presented the whole Minoan civilization in a way to fit his laws of rout and rally. Etc."

Was it true that he was preparing a piece about Carr for *Encounter?*

"I am reviewing 'What Is History?' at length," he said. "It is not a good book. Carr presents his own side with an enormous degree of sophistication, whilst his opponents are ridiculed. For example, he denigrates the role of accident in history by saying that people who argue from accident are arguing from the shape of Cleopatra's nose, or the proverbial monkey bite that killed the king. They are saying, 'Were it not for the shape of Cleopatra's nose, or the monkey bite that killed the king, the course of history would have been different.' Suppose we substitute for Cleopatra's nose the death of Churchill in 1939. Am I then to be told by the Carrs of this world that the course of history would have gone on pretty much as it did under the leadership of Churchill? For my other criticisms of Carr, I direct you to my *Encounter* review, which will be on the stands in a month or two."

Were there any twentieth-century English historians he admired?

"Not really."

"Not even Tawney or Namier?" I asked. In the eyes of many professional historians in Britain, R. H. Tawney is considered to be second only to Sir Lewis Namier. The two men, it is thought, revolutionized the study of history — one by brilliantly employing economic analysis, the other by using psychological and biographical tools. It is said that Tawney and Namier did for history what Marx and Freud had done for sociology and psychology, respectively.

"A colleague of Tawney's told me the other day,"

Trevor-Roper said, "that he used to get very emotional about evidence which contradicted his theories. He sometimes valued his conclusions too much. I do admire Namier, though I think his method is a limited one."

"Whom do you admire unreservedly?" I asked.

"Gibbon."

"In this century?"

"One or two French historians."

"Do you have any theories of history yourself?" I asked.

"Yes. I believe in parallels in history — what happened in the fourth century B.C. can throw light on the twentieth century. I believe in the law of causation — x causes y in history."

His credo was so unexceptionable that neither Tawney nor Namier nor Toynbee nor Taylor nor Carr would argue with it.

"Sometimes," I said, a little cautiously, "you explain away the works of men like Toynbee and Taylor in terms of their prejudices. Are there any personal details about you that could throw light on your way of writing history?"

"Not really," he said.

As soon as I had left Trevor-Roper, I got hold of a set of proofs of his *Encounter* article, which was called "E. H. Carr's Success Story." Like many other reviewers, Trevor-Roper took the Cambridge historian to task for his determinism (Carr had dismissed the people who tarried over the might-have-beens of history as players of a "parlour-game"); for his new definition of the "objective" historian (believing that historians were not free from prejudice, Carr had to some degree redefined objectivity in a historian, as "the capacity to project his vision into the future"); and for disregarding accidents and contingencies. But the weight of Trevor-Roper's axe fell on Carr personally. Here, as in his other *Encounter* executions, the condemned man's personal life was made the scapegoat for some of his views (this time with the emphasis on Carr's proposition, "Study the historian before you begin to study the facts").

In 1939 [Trevor-Roper wrote], Mr. Carr published an important book, "The Twenty Years' Crisis," in which he appeared, as so often since, as a "realist," cutting as ruthlessly through the "utopian," "idealist" verbiage of Sir Alfred Zimmern and Dr. Lauterpacht as he now cuts through the antiquated liberalism of Sir Isaiah Berlin and Dr. Popper. The upshot of his argument was that only the realities of power matter, and that German power, and the ideas to which it gave force, must be respected as a *datum* in politics. The book was, as Mr. A. J. P. Taylor has recently called it, "a brilliant argument in favour of appeasement." A few years later, Mr. Carr changed his mind about the realities of power, and during the war, when he contributed largely to *The Times*, he became known as "the Red Professor of Printing House Square." But suppose that, in the 1930s, he had written a history of Germany, "objective" in his sense of the word, according to the evolving standard "laid up in the future," and disregarding "the might-have-beens of history." I have no doubt it would have been a brilliant work, lucid, trenchant, profound. No doubt it would have been acute in analysis and without crude error or misjudgment. Nevertheless, I wonder how well it would have worn: how "objective," in any sense of the word, it would have appeared to us now, when the Nazi success story has ended in discredit and failure. In fact Mr. Carr did not write a history of Germany. But his great "History of Soviet Russia" bears the same relation to "What Is History?" which that unwritten history would presumably have borne to "The Twenty Years' Crisis." For what is the most obvious characteristic of "A History of Soviet Russia"? It is the author's unhesitating identification of history with the victorious cause, his ruthless dismissal of its opponents, of its victims, and of all who did not stay on, or steer, the bandwagon. The "might-have-beens," the deviationists, the rivals, the critics of Lenin are reduced to insignificance, denied justice, or hearing, or space, because they backed the wrong horse. History proved them wrong, and the historian's essential task is to take the side of History. . . . No historian since the crudest ages of clerical bigotry has treated evidence with such dogmatic ruthlessness as this. No historian, even in those ages, has exalted such dogmatism into an historiographical theory. As Sir Isaiah Berlin wrote in his review of Mr. Carr's first volume (and perhaps it is this as much as the arguments in "Historical Inevitability" which has provoked Mr. Carr to pursue him so pertinaciously through these pages): "If Mr. Carr's remaining volumes equal this impressive opening, they will constitute the most monumental challenge of our time to that ideal of impartiality and objective truth and even-handed justice in the writing of history which is most deeply embedded in the European liberal tradition."

Impressed as I was by Trevor-Roper's ability to aim his bullets at the most vulnerable parts of his prey, to find chinks in everybody's armor, I put down "E. H.

Carr's Success Story" in a state of exasperation. Trevor-Roper had a gift for marshalling the faults of a historian — a Toynbee, a Taylor, a Carr — without a grain of sympathy. After reading him, one wondered why the books had been written at all, why anyone read them, why anyone took them seriously. He put me in mind of a literary critic who has no love for writers, whose criticism is not an enhancement of our understanding, an invitation to read the book again in the light of his interpretation, but simply an instrument of destruction. Yet the paradox was that in principle Trevor-Roper seemed to have no objection to historians who, in error, put forward challenging theses. He had written once in a lecture, "Think of the great controversies launched by Henri Pirenne's famous thesis on Mohammed and Charlemagne. No one now accepts it in the form in which he published it. But how the living interest in Europe's dark ages was re-created by the challenge which he uttered and the controversy which he engendered! Think too of Max Weber's famous thesis on the Protestant ethic: a thesis of startling simplicity and — in my opinion — demonstrable error. But how much poorer our understanding of the Reformation, how much feebler our interest in it would be today, if that challenge had not been thrown down, and taken up! The greatest professional historians of our century . . . have always been those who have applied to historical study not merely the exact, professional discipline they have learned within it but also the sciences, the hypotheses, the human interest which — however intermixed with human error — have been brought into it by the lay world outside."

Perhaps the explanation of Trevor-Roper's Janus-like posture, scowling at Pirennes and Webers with one face, smiling at them with the other, lay not with him but with England. Even as I had been chasing the Hydra of historical and philosophical controversy, the intellectual atmosphere in Britain was thickening with hundreds of other altercations until the air choked with a miasmic, blinding fog. In a sense, to follow any of the proliferating controversies to its roots was to discover oneself writing about the intellectual life of a people. Going for the largest game, creating an intellectual sensation, striking a posture, sometimes at the expense of truth, stating the arguments against a book or its author in the most relentless, sometimes violent way, engaging the interest of practically the whole intelligentsia by using every nook and cranny of journalism, carrying on a bitter war of words in public but keeping friendships intact in private, generally enjoying the fun of going against the grain — all these features prominent in historical disputation were also part of the broader English mental scene. The more secure the castle of any reputation, the more battering rams arrived to assail it, and Sir Charles Snow and Dr. F. R. Leavis were but the most spectacular casualties of what Hampshire in the *New Statesman* called "a ruinous conflict." The role of the papers themselves in many of these personal or intellectual conflicts

could be glimpsed in the *Spectator's* first publishing the
acrimonious and ruinous utterances of Leavisites and
Snowites and then closing the controversy with an editorial that began, "Controversy on matters of intellectual
principle frequently has the disadvantage of obscuring
those issues which it is intended to lay bare." I had not
read all the volumes of "A Study of History," or actually
agreed with "The Origins of the Second World War," or
carefully listened for the thunder of the big battalions
in Carr's monumental work on Russia, or probably
grasped the full implications of "What Is History?," but
I had read enough of, and thought enough about, many
of the works to be excited by them, and to be interested
in these historians as men.

My next visit was to Arnold Toynbee, who works in
Chatham House, in London — the home of the Royal
Institute of International Affairs.

I arrived at the two-hundred-year-old house early one
afternoon, and was shown by a watchful porter to a door
on the second floor marked rather portentously "The
Toynbee Room," but the professor who opened the door
was anything but portentous. Toynbee, who is seventy-
three, is a medium-sized, alert-looking man with a heavy
head and a heavy nose. He was wearing an old blue
serge suit, which hung rather loosely around him, and
he suggested a saint who is wrapped up in his theories
and his prayers and yet is eager to please. The Toynbee
Room appeared to be a shrine not so much to him as

to a world long past. Books on archeology, on ancient Greece and Rome, on China, on Egypt, on the Orient were spread out like panel after panel of mosaics in a cathedral. Over the fireplace was a portrait of Toynbee.

"Oh," he said of this, rather apologetically, looking away from it, "I used to have a rather good print of the Parthenon there, but my elder son presented me with this painting and . . ."

There wasn't a single volume on the twentieth century, and when I commented on this, Toynbee said simply, "I keep all the modern books at home. I will be leaving those to the family. These more valuable ones I am leaving to Chatham House."

We sat facing each other in a corner and talked.

I asked Toynbee how he managed to produce one thick volume almost each year.

"I have a very good memory, but it sits lightly on me," he said. "I read an enormous amount, but I suppose it's from experience that I know exactly what to copy down in my ruled, ten-by-six notebooks I have a sort of foreknowledge about useful material. Sometimes I take notes years in advance of actually writing a book. I have just been in Italy in connection with a study on ancient Rome, for which I have been unsystematically taking notes for the last forty-odd years. Whenever I come across an interesting quotation, I copy it out in one of my notebooks, and I have now filled twenty-five of them. Incidentally, I have sold my notebooks, along with the longhand text of 'A Study of History,' to the manuscript collector Arthur Houghton, of Corning Glass. If it doesn't bore you, I was in America recently, and called on Houghton and found some of my writings, framed, alongside some by Alexander Pope, who has an exquisite hand. It was like returning from the dead." He laughed quietly.

"How did you come to write your 'Study of History'?" I asked.

"It all goes back to the First World War," Toynbee answered readily. "I happened to be rereading Thucydides' 'Peloponnesian War,' when it struck me that the tragic experience we were going through had already been experienced by the Greeks. It came to me that it was possible for one society to have experienced things — such as a mortal war — that were still in the future for another society. Two societies could be spaced wide apart chronologically and yet be mentally contemporaneous. I have been at work on the 'Study' ever since."

With time banished as a factor from the life of a society, Toynbee said, a human mind could compare and contrast the experiences of various societies and make some fruitful, scientifically valid generalizations about man's experience in the universe. From the very beginning, he went on, his whole enterprise had been precarious. There was the antipathetic climate of opinion, the depression, the war, and a race with his own life cycle. He had written his book under tremendous mental pressure, and it was only by chance that it was not killed before its inception. "In 1911," Toynbee explained, "I came down from Balliol and made straight for Greece. I spent a year there, tramping about the villages, talking to anybody and everybody, generally learning about Greece. I had an inaccurate Austrian staff map with me, which, among the other howlers, indicated a nonexistent road. I thought I'd found it, and, being thirsty, drank a lot of the roadside water, until a Greek shouted across to me, 'You shouldn't drink that water, it's *bad* water!' Because of the bad water, I contracted dysentery, which took years to throw off, but because of the dysentery I was not a second lieutenant in the war, and did not, like half my college contemporaries, die in it. Isn't it extraordinary how chance does work in history?"

"If you believe in chance," I asked, "how can you believe in historical laws?"

"I don't think I am a determinist," Toynbee said. "I believe in free will. I often think back to the intervention of chance, like the death of Alexander the Great. Had he not died young, he might have politically united the world. Today, instead of two warring camps, we might have had a united world, with no nuclear sword of Damocles over our heads."

"But if one chance can affect history so," I insisted, "then — "

"Ah, yes!" he interrupted. "But Alexander the Great is an exception. In his case, no other Alexander came along to do the job. In most cases, there are many candidates, and it's a matter of chance who does the job, who gets the recognition. Many people had the idea of evolution simultaneously in the nineteenth century, *because the time was ripe,* but Charles Darwin got the recognition."

Granted that, so to speak, human fruits did ripen and rot according to the seasons of civilizations, how had Toynbee had the audacity to formulate climatic laws from only a couple of dozen specimen societies?

"I would, of course, have liked hundreds and thousands of specimen civilizations to work from, but I did the best I could with the samples I had," Toynbee replied immediately. "Charles Darwin says somewhere that 'ten specimens are too many for a scientist.'"

All the criticisms and reconsiderations, Toynbee said, had not shaken his fundamental belief that human experience has a pattern, a shape, an order; indeed, he had anticipated, in 1919, when he first outlined his magnum opus, all the criticism that was later heaped on his head. Today he stood alone as a grand generalizer, but he comforted himself with the thought that the days of the microscope historians were probably numbered. They, whether they admitted it or not, had sacrificed all generalizations for patchwork, relative knowledge, and they thought of human experience as incomprehensible chaos. But in the perspective of historiography, they were in the minority, and Toynbee, in company with St. Augustine — he felt most akin to him — Polybius, Roger Bacon, and Ibn Khaldun, was in the majority. "You see," Toynbee said, "I was a scholar at Winchester, and naturally subjected to all sorts of tribal customs. I fought many of the customs, and you can, I think, explain away some of my differences with the contemporary historians — I am a minority of one — by saying I am still going against the grain, against the tribal customs."

"But Augustine and Bacon weren't going against the current of their times — they were going with it," I said. "Indeed, they epitomized the spirit of their times."

"That's true," Toynbee said. "But then there are many other men whose work was only recognized years after their death. I think, you see, that history moves in alternations." At the moment, he went on, we were passing through a despairing time in intellectual matters, but a period of generalization was not necessarily not just around the corner. In any case, he had not neglected the mood of the century completely. He had kept his feet on the ground of our times by producing "Survey of International Affairs," a series of yearly studies for the Royal Institute of International Affairs. From the very start of his "Study," he had entertained no hopes for it in his lifetime. "As soon as I put pen to paper," he said, "I knew that whatever reputation I had would go up in smoke." The first two three-volume sets of his "Study," in fact, had been published and forgotten in the shadow of the Second World War. The postwar volumes had been written in a slightly different mood — as a sort of tract for the times. He had tried to do for history what Jung had done for psychology. Both he and Jung, as more historical and psychological facts came to light, would be superseded, as a matter of course, but as far as he was concerned, if even a quarter of his generalizations were not lost in the sands of time, he would consider his work well done. He and Jung had come upon their ideas separately — not a small portent of the times. Jung's discovery of psychological types, primordial images, Toynbee said, was very similar to his discovery of contemporaneous societies. "You know, Jung served in the Swiss artillery," Toynbee went on. "Once, his unit was digging a trench in the Alps. They had been digging hard for some time when an artilleryman shouted, in exasperation, 'If we dig any farther, we will come to the *Mothers.*'"

Some critics, he added, had accused him, Toynbee, of finding not just the bed of civilizations under the mountain of facts but gods as well; Mothers and civilizations were one thing, gods another. But if the death of civilizations did give rise to religions, how could he help applauding their death, especially since the better off a civilization was materially, the less vital it was spiritually?

"Since I do not believe in a personal god," Toynbee went on, "I don't have a vested interest in any one religion. If it doesn't bore you . . . Although, of course, I can't get away from my Judaeo-Christian background, temperamentally I am a Hindu. As a Hindu, I don't have any difficulty in believing in many gods simultaneously, or thinking that a syncretist faith may be the answer for our age. To Hindus, it's of no consequence which road, Siva or Vishnu, one travels — all roads lead to Heaven."

I asked Toynbee if his religious views had provided

the motive and the cue for Trevor-Roper's violent attack.

"If it doesn't bore you," he said, "I have been very puzzled by that article. If Trevor-Roper thought my ideas to be rubbish, why did he bother with them, and that, too, in such a systematic and relentless fashion? When the onslaught was published, *Encounter* pressed me to write an answer, but I'm pleased that I didn't adopt my enemy's tactics. In the original version of the 'Reconsiderations,' I said quite a few harsh things about Trevor-Roper, but my wife edited them out, and I'm glad. For, you see, Trevor-Roper, by overelectrocuting me, really electrocuted himself. Of course, he hurt me very much — I still feel pain in my pinched tail — but . . ."

Taking up the cudgels for him, I said, "You could safely have made short work of his comparison of you to Hitler."

"Did he compare me to Hitler?" Toynbee asked with innocent surprise. "Oh, I'd forgotten that. I may be forced to write another volume of answers." He laughed. "And then I shall certainly disclaim being a Hitler."

"Another volume!" I said.

"Well, Pieter Geyl, my very pugnacious and persistent critic" — Toynbee's tone was affectionate — "brought out a pamphlet answering and dismissing my 'Reconsiderations' practically within ten days of its publication. So far, I've only written him a remonstrating letter, but if he goes on at this rate, I may well have to bring out another book of answers." After a pause, he said, "By the way, what did you think was the most damaging count in Trevor-Roper's indictment — in case I *should* write another 'Reconsiderations'?"

"I thought his quotations from your autobiographical, tenth volume were quite telling," I said.

"It may sound to you like double-talk," Toynbee said, reconsidering, "but I don't really believe in objective history, so in the autobiographical volume I tried to put on the table my environment, my prejudices, and my methods — the bag of tools I used in writing the 'Study.' Often when reading historians like Thucydides I have missed not having a record of their lives and training. Such a record would certainly have illuminated their works for me. I think it's a help to the readers of my 'Study' to know that my mother was a historian, my elder sister is a professor of archeology at Cambridge, my younger sister is an excellent monographer on the Stuart dynasty, one of my sons, Philip, is a distinguished literary critic, and so on. Even Philip's novel 'Pantaloon' — it is largely autobiographical — might aid some curious future readers."

"But surely Trevor-Roper is complaining about the autobiographical excesses rather than about the facts," I said.

"Yes," Toynbee promptly agreed. "I wrote 'A Study of History' under enormous mental pressure. All the while I was writing it, I didn't know if there was time enough in the world to finish it. Also" — he hesitated —

"I wrote some of those volumes under fire, when I was having lots of trouble. You see, my first marriage had collapsed, affecting me deeply, and . . . in a sense, I never got over it. A tired man is apt to make mistakes."

I wanted to talk to him about the many historians I had been reading, but he had not seen Taylor's book and had not heard of Carr's "What Is History?" He readily admitted not knowing much about the professional historians, but he thought he admired Miss Wedgwood and Tawney. "I am very ignorant about their fields, however, so I suppose I can't really judge them," he said. "Before you censure me for my ignorance of day-to-day history, I ought to tell you that the climate of my mind is wholly classical. It's because of a classical education that I've concentrated all my energies on looking for order in human experience."

"But Trevor-Roper had a classical education," I said.

"Oh, I didn't know that," he said. "I can't imagine, then, what he got out of it. I am not saying that a classical education stamps people with a uniform point of view but, rather, that it does endow men with some common properties. Gibbon had a point of view totally opposite from mine, but nevertheless, because of his classical education, I can read him with pleasure, just as I think he could read me with pleasure."

"Would Trevor-Roper grant Gibbon's reading you with pleasure?" I asked.

"Perhaps not," Toynbee said, laughing.

It was nearly seven, and Toynbee asked me to dine

with him at the Athenæum, a club that is said to have
more bishops per square inch than any other club in the
world. "I very seldom go out," he said, "but I warned
my wife in advance that I might take you to my club
today." He said that, aside from his family, he didn't
see many people. He had lunch once a week with one
old school friend, a retired county judge, and sometimes he met a retired insurance executive. Out on the
street, he didn't so much walk as float on a thick cushion
of air, and he gave the impression of being a Gabriel
among the people.

In the club, Toynbee ordered medium-dry sherry,
lentil soup, steak and kidney pie, and strawberry ice, and
talked rather expansively about a seventeen-month
journey he had taken around the world a little while
back as a journalist, which had resulted in a book called
"Between Oxus and Jumna." "When I travel," he said,
"I carry in my pocket a copy of the Bhagavad-Gita, a
volume of Dante, an anthology of the metaphysical poets,
and 'Faust' — books I read over and over again. Some
people live by Freud and 'Hamlet.' I live by Jung and
'Faust.'"

Toynbee's attempt to generalize, his regarding history
as a tapestry with recurring patterns, his ordering of the
life of a civilization according to its religion and art (the
development of medicine and science, the basis for most
people's belief in human progress, hardly gets a hearing
in his work — no wonder the West has been on the de-

cline since the sixteenth century), his refusal to believe
that the faith of ages past in an orderly world has been
shattered like a Humpty-Dumpty, never to be put together again — all are contrary to the predominant mood.
This, perhaps, is the reason Toynbee has attracted critics
as a sweetshop invites children. The most formidable
of the living critics, possibly, is Pieter Geyl, of the University of Utrecht. Geyl, who is seventy-five, spent more
than twenty years (1913-35) in England, beginning as a
correspondent for a Dutch newspaper and then becom-
ing a professor — first of Dutch studies and then of Dutch
history — at London University. He is well acquainted
with — indeed, a part of — the English historical scene,
and his reputation among the professionals is as high as
Toynbee's is low. A. J. P. Taylor, who is almost as sparing
of compliments as Trevor-Roper, and almost as prolific
as Toynbee, wrote a rapturous piece about Geyl for his
seventieth birthday: "When people ask impatiently:
'How then would you define an historian?' I am at no
loss for an answer. This is my definition: Pieter Geyl is
an historian. . . . He represents the ideal towards which
historians strive — or rather (to avoid generalizing in my
turn) towards which I, as an historian, strive and towards which other historians whom I admire strive
also. . . . Even when he is wrong (and I think he is
sometimes), he is wrong as only an historian can be. . . .
The historical significance of Dr. Geyl's work (much of
which has been translated into English) has been widely
acknowledged; this year its literary significance, too, was

recognized, when he was chosen to receive the P. C. Hooft Prize, the leading Dutch literary award. . . . His style is unassertive. But when he has reached the point of decision, his words fall like the blows of a hammer. . . . His attitude towards historical evidence is well seen in his prolonged controversy with Toynbee. Faced with a sweeping generalization covering the centuries, Geyl does not intervene with an equally generalized doubt. Modestly, unassumingly, he takes some individual case — the rise of the Netherlands, the British colonies in North America, the unification of Italy — and asks: 'Does the generalization accord with these facts?' When it does not, that is the end so far as Geyl is concerned." Taylor then, as a professional historian, used the occasion to discharge some volleys at Toynbee. "But that is not the end for Toynbee," he wrote. "It is not even the beginning; it is nothing at all. For, since he makes up generalizations to suit his convenience or his religious whim of the moment, the fact that they do not accord with the evidence is irrelevant to him." This was not all. Geyl could not even comprehend the workings of Toynbee's mind: "He [Geyl] cannot bring himself to believe that anyone should fly so willfully and so persistently in the face of evidence as Toynbee does. Therefore Geyl comes back once more to wrestle with the convicted sinner, hopeful that — this time — he will see the light. But it is of no avail. Toynbee remains incorrigible; and once more the damning sentence is pronounced." And, Taylor continued, "the same rigorous appeal to the evidence is

shown in the historical work with which Geyl made his
name. He challenged the accepted version of how the
Netherlands were divided. Earlier historians had explained the division by differences of religion or of race
or of national character. They did not find these differences in the historical evidence; they put the differences in from their own experience or inclinations. Dutch
Protestants wanted to show that Holland had always
been predominantly Protestant and that Protestantism
was a superior religion. Belgian historians wanted to
show that Belgium had always existed as an independent
entity, though no one noticed this at the time. Geyl
looked at the evidence. He studied the contemporary
record and noticed the obvious things which no one had
noticed before: the decisive part played by the Spanish
army and the line of the great rivers. This is a less in-
spiring and romantic explanation than the older ones;
it is less flattering to national pride, whether Dutch or
Belgian. It has only the virtue of happening to be cor-
rect; and it is now difficult to imagine a time when men
did not realize it. The discrediting of the older version
and the substitution of a better one, firmly based on evidence, is one of the most beautiful historical operations
in our lifetime."

With Taylor's tribute as my guide — he seemed to be
leading me out of the medieval, theological world of
Toynbee and into the modern, medical world of Geyl —
I made my way to Utrecht to see the Dutch historian.
One of his pupils, who met me at my hotel, the Pays-

Bas, the morning I arrived, told me a little bit about him. "Both Geyl's father and his grandfather were doctors," his pupil told me, "and while his mind still has the precision of an operating room, as a man he is vain as only a humanist can be. Once, in a seminar, a student argued that one day national barriers might disappear, leaving the world with one state and one language. Geyl pounced on him: 'But what about my immortal Dutch prose?' It was said with a touch of irony, but only a *touch* of irony. Some of his works, even now, he won't have translated, saying, 'If anyone wants to know what I think, he can jolly well learn Dutch.' In fact, I believe he's somewhat hostile to the Common Market because he fears that the Dutch language will disappear in such an organization. This is not just love of the language but love of his country and its history. In that sort of way, he is very much a conservative."

After some lunch, I went to Geyl's house. I knew it was a Hollander's home by the bicycles in the doorway. Geyl, who opened the door, proved to be an impressive gentleman — a tall man with the gray beard of the wise and the narrow smile of the aristocrat. He was wearing an unobtrusive hearing aid, a blue tie, an English-style gray jacket, and gray trousers. He invited me to follow him up a narrow wooden stairway, and showed me into his study. It was as thick with books as the Toynbee Room, but Geyl's books had a distinctly modern look. Behind his desk was a two-shelf display of various editions and translations of his works. He picked out the smallest volume, his English translation of the four-teenth-century Dutch play "Lancelot of Denmark," and, holding it close to his heart, read aloud, in a soft English:

> "Now hear what we intend to play.
> 'Tis all about a valiant knight,
> Who loved a lady day and night.
> Noble of heart she was and pure,
> But of lowly birth for very sure."

Returning the book to the shelf, he said, "How I've loved history!" We sat down under what Geyl told me was his favorite print of his mentor, Erasmus, and near the window, which looked out on the Biltse Straatweg — a road along which, in the Second World War, the Dutch Army had retreated and then the liberating Canadian Army had advanced.

"I am by nature a talker," Geyl began, "and unless somebody baits me, making me angry, I tend to go on talking. Do you mind?"

I said no indeed.

"Until my chance encounter with Toynbee," Geyl said, "I rather prided myself on my ignorance about the philosophy of history; he made me take my first step toward wisdom by regretting my ignorance. My fame as a philosopher of history is not only accidental but gratuitous. Toynbee has done for me in the historical world what Margot Fonteyn did for me at Oxford." He pointed to a picture on the opposite wall, which showed him, tall and serious in an academic gown, beside the graceful and striking Margot Fonteyn, also in an academic gown. "She and I received honorary degrees at Oxford the same year," Geyl said. "When we walked through the streets in academic procession, no one had eyes for anybody but her. I was her neighbor, and because of that I was noticed. I encountered Toynbee when an English journalist who was visiting me here in 1946 asked me if I'd heard of 'A Study of History.' I said I hadn't. Out of politeness, he sent me as much of it as had been published. I was struck by the first half of what I read, but by the second half I was completely disenchanted. In the meantime, Jan Romein — he is a historical materialist, and thinks that all unphilosophical historians are helpless sailors on the sea of history, while historical philosophers like himself and Toynbee are the captains — was using it as part of his seminar in a rival Dutch university. I decided to bait him a little, and did so by making Toynbee's determinism the subject of an attack in a paper I delivered before our national Historical Association. The B.B.C. must have got wind of my argument with Romein, for it invited me to debate with Toynbee on the Third Programme. I faced Toynbee on the wireless, and accused him of dipping into the caldron of facts and taking only those which fitted his theories. He said all historians approached facts with theories, and if they denied this, they were simply ignorant of the workings of their own minds. I said all systems were doomed to disappointment. He said people who believed that took the view that history was nonsense. I said no, they didn't. So it went. When the remainder of his 'Study' came out, I flayed him for finding a panacea for our troubles in a universal religion. In 'Reconsiderations' he made me 'the spokesman of the jury.' He said I had been 'plaintively asking for answers.' 'Plaintively' is not quite the word." Geyl smiled his narrow smile. "I demolished his 'Reconsiderations' with a pamphlet," he continued. "The trouble with Toynbee is that, because of his religion, he will not acquiesce, like us secularists, in human ignorance. Like Faust, he tries to know more than can be known. I was saved from Toynbee's religion and Toynbee's fate by a priest. When I was eleven or twelve, I wandered into a cathedral and found myself in the middle of Vespers. I started going there every day about six o'clock — mostly for the music, I suppose. One day, a priest came up to me and put his hand on my shoulder and said, 'Little boy — ' I raced out of the cathedral and have never returned." He brought out of his pocket a copy of what he told me was the only sonnet he had ever written in English. "This sonnet," he said, tapping the piece of paper, "composed in a concentration camp, contains my philosophy, and colors my historical thinking." Without a pause, he rushed through the sonnet:

> "The stars are fright'ning. The cold universe,
> Boundless and silent, goes revolving on,
> Worlds without end. The grace of God is gone.
> A vast indifference, deadlier than a curse,
> Chills our poor globe, which Heaven seemed to nurse
> So fondly. 'Twas God's rainbow when it shone,
> Until we searched. Now, as we count and con
> Gusts of infinity, our hopes disperse.

Well, if it's so, then turn your eyes away
From Heav'n. Look at the earth, in its array
Of life and beauty. — Transitory? Maybe,
But so are you. Let stark eternity
Heed its own self, and you, enjoy your day,
And when death calls, then quietly obey."

He sighed. "How I wish I could argue Toynbee out of some of his ideas!" he said. Then, abruptly changing the subject, he asked, "Have you read Carr's 'What Is History?' — this year's Trevelyan lectures?"

I said I had.

"Well," he announced, "I am giving the Trevelyan lectures next year. They will probably be on Dutch history and my historical revolution, which Taylor has called 'one of the most beautiful historical operations in our lifetime.' Good heavens, if I had accepted some of the theoretical pronouncements of my Trevelyan predecessor, my operation probably couldn't have been performed at all. And if anyone had taken seriously — thanks to me, not many people did — historians like Toynbee, who go in for simple explanations of things, the result would have been much the same."

I asked him to say more about this.

"Carr, in his lectures, gives no role to fortuitous events," he said. "But, good heavens, the division of the sixteenth-century Netherlands into Holland, in the north, and Belgium, in the south — what was it if not fortuitous? You know, before the sixteenth century all this area was one Netherlands. But the Spaniards succeeded in holding on to only the southern half. Before my revolution, it was thought that the Spaniards were unable to subdue the rebellious northern provinces because of the difference between the Flemish and Dutch temperaments. The southerners, the Flemings, were flighty, frivolous, lighthearted — an easy prey to Catholicism. The northerners were serious, hard-working, commercial-minded, and Calvinist — therefore not an easy prey to Catholicism. My revolution consisted in advancing a simple military explanation in place of all this abstract theory. I said the reason the Spaniards didn't subjugate the north was that they were stopped by the great rivers — the Rhine and the Meuse. My discovery was borne out by General Montgomery, eight, nine months before the end of the European phase of the Second World War, when he, too, was stopped, at the Battle of Arnhem, by the *fortuitous* rivers. You see the dangers of imposing theories on facts?"

Geyl paused, and I nodded.

"The infuriating thing about Toynbee, a historical materialist like Romein, a determinist like Carr is that they believe in laws," Geyl continued. "But I say — you'll find it in my book 'Napoleon: For and Against' — that history is an argument without end." We could agree, he said, about simple facts — the Second World War began in 1939 — but such facts were a very small part of history; the rest was made up of judgments of events, situations, and characters, and *they* would be debated till doomsday. "In my 'Napoleon,'" Geyl went on, "I surveyed all the century-and-a-half-old arguments about Napoleon. What historians from generation to generation thought about him — whether in their eyes he was in or out — depended, it turned out, upon the politics of the time. Have you read the book?"

I said I had, and remembered well the famous "Argument" passage:

"To expect from history those final conclusions, which may perhaps be obtained in other disciplines, is, in my opinion, to misunderstand its nature. . . . The scientific method serves above all to establish facts; there is a great deal about which we can reach agreement by its use. But as soon as there is a question of explanation, of interpretation, of appreciation, though the special method of the historian remains valuable, the personal element can no longer be ruled out — that point of view which is determined by the circumstances of his time and by his own preconceptions. . . . Truth, though for God it may be One, assumes many shapes to men. Thus it is that the analysis of so many conflicting opinions concerning one historical phenomenon is not just a means of whiling away the time, nor need it lead to discouraging conclusions concerning the untrustworthiness of historical study. The study even of contradictory conceptions can be fruitful. . . . History is indeed an argument without end."

With a smile, he now added, "Good heavens, if there were such a thing as objective history, people would have made up their minds about Napoleon long ago."

Like a good lecturer, Geyl read the questions in my mind and, instead of my putting them to him, put them to me. "Have you read Taylor's 'Origins of the Second World War'?" he asked.

I said I had.

"I pasted that book in a review," he said proudly, "and, through correspondence, have been arguing with him about his thesis ever since. In his letters to me he says that, contrary to all the allegations, he has not gone out of his way to provoke, to create a sensation, to confound everybody with paradoxes. He says he wrote the book with truth and objectivity as his only touchstones. He says he objectively discovered Hitler to be just another statesman. He insists Hitler was a godsend, for if anybody more shrewd than Hitler had come along, he might have dominated Europe without a war. He says his book is not an apology for Chamberlain, not an apology for the policy of appeasement, but simply an explanation of them. I say, what is an explanation if not an apology? I wrote to him insisting that Hitler was not just another statesman but a unique phenomenon. I said that he, Taylor, had been too faithful to his printed documents, that he had overlooked the temper of Germany in the thirties — the street gangs, the S.S., the S.A., the whole Nazi phenomenon. I said that to write about Hitler and the war as though it were all a natural consequence of the Treaty of Versailles, and leave out of the calculation Hitler the freak of nature, dynamism gone mad, and the reasons for his success — the acute depression and the complete collapse of the economy in the early thirties — was bad history. I insisted that a historian was inevitably limited by his time, his period, his situation, and that there was no such thing as objective history. To make my point, I sent him copies of my correspondence with my intimate friend Carel Gerretson —I am going to include them in a small volume of my letters."

Geyl was by now as excited as a lecturer at the climax of an oration. Getting up, he feverishly rummaged in his desk for the Gerretson letters, without, however, stopping the flow of his words. He told me that Gerretson was a Dutch poet, historian, and politician, and he explained the context of one particular letter. It was written in 1939 and concerned one Dr. Hendrik Krekel, who was a journalist. "You see," Geyl said, "when a Hague daily stopped publishing Krekel's weekly reviews of the international situation, Krekel collected some of them and brought them out in pamphlet form. Gerretson forwarded the pamphlet to me, challenging me to deny that the reviews were models of objectivity, fair-mindedness, and good journalism. What I wrote" — interrupting himself to exclaim "Here it is!," he triumphantly fished out of a drawer the relevant letter to Gerretson — "about Krekel then applies just as much to the sort of history Taylor writes." He read, in a loud, clear voice, " 'Krekel's expositions no doubt have their interest. There is something attractive in this method of systematically connecting events with earlier phases; the writer has a keen mind.

But objective? When a man writes in a quiet and matter-of-fact way, avoids the use of big words, does not betray any emotion or express any sympathy, letting his conclusions or opinions appear only in the most moderate terms or even obliquely — that does not make him objective. Krekel does not waste words on the moral worth, or, let me say, on the anti-moral, anti-human tendencies of the German regime; at most, he mentions them once in a while when he notices that the horror evoked by them elsewhere constitutes a factor. The feverishness inherent in every dictatorship, the need to register successes, the absence of all counterweight of criticism — all such factors Krekel leaves out of account in his estimates, or at least does not give them their due weight. In this I see the symptoms of a feeling of affinity with the German system, or of moral blindness; at any rate, no objectivity. Those elements must be taken into account in every higher synthesis. To keep talking all the time in terms of power politics, imperialism versus imperialism — let it be in itself as able and well-informed as you please, it denotes a one-sidedness which must lead to formidable miscalculations.'" Putting the letter down, Geyl said, "How true all this is of Taylor! Krekel and Taylor not only are trying to do the impossible but are gravely erring. Taylor is still writing old-fashioned political history, from which it appears that the great issues of the world are settled in Foreign Offices rather than in society at large." Some aspects of Taylor's history, Geyl said, had an all too imposing ancestry in Sir Lewis Namier's work.

Namier all of the time and Taylor much of the time had no *real* respect for statesmen and policies, ideas and ideologies, which for them, as for Freud, were simply reflexes — responses to subconscious influences. Because of its purely factual approach, Namier-Taylor history had a kind of pointedness, a kind of dramatic quality, a kind of brilliance; in their hands history took wings as only good stories did, but their picture of the society was no more than a bird's-eye view of it.

For the first time, Geyl's voice became freighted with emotion. Until then, he had been talking like a European professor, who is more used to lecturing than to holding tutorials or seminars. His arguments were clear and limpid, but one felt that they had already taken place, rather than — as in a good tutorial or seminar — that they were still in the future. Now he seemed a little confused, as though he were still debating something in his mind.

" 'The Origins of the Second World War' is dreadful history," Geyl said. "But Taylor has eulogized me — you've seen his article on my seventieth birthday?"

I said I had.

"Well, then," he said, "it would be only reasonable that I should have agreed to contribute to a *Festschrift* that a man at Oxford is organizing for him. But I refused. Do you think I was right? Or — "

Just then we were interrupted by a red-cheeked woman, only a little shorter than Geyl, who came in carrying a couple of cups of tea. She introduced herself as his wife, and said as she handed us the tea, "I hope my husband found all the books and papers he needed. He is so untidy that I don't know what he would do without me." With that, she left us.

"I don't know what I would do without her," Geyl echoed. "We used to bicycle a lot before the Utrecht traffic got so heavy. Now we pass the time playing draughts."

I asked Geyl a question that had been troubling me for some time — how controversy could be a way to the truth. In return, he told me a story. "During the Second World War," he said, "the great French historian Lucien Febvre proposed that, to keep the spirits of the French youth high, they should be encouraged to read Jules Michelet, the Romantic historian. Michelet was intensely nationalistic. He always talked about 'the great French nation;' for him, France was the *crème de la crème* of nations. In one of my essays, I attacked Febvre for his Micheletism. When Febvre came to Utrecht, a friend invited me to lunch with him, and I went, prepared for a good intellectual fight about Michelet. But when I broached the subject, he simply said, 'I do not wish to discuss it.'" Geyl produced his narrow, aristocratic smile. "Good heavens, what future is there to history if you take that attitude? For me, as I've said, history is an argument without end, and temperamentally I am a born polemicist — but not, of course, on the scale of Trevor-Roper."

Geyl's mind, perhaps, was like Trevor-Roper's, I thought, but as a man he streamed with a charm no less

engulfing than Toynbee's; even his vanity and his haugh-
tiness were engaging. It was easy to see how in argument he could get the better of Toynbee. But Carr and
Taylor were different matters. There was much more to
Carr than his theory about fortuitous events, and from
the little history I knew, it seemed to me, judging Geyl
in accordance with his dictum — "A historian is inevitably
limited by his time, period, situation" — that some of his
strong feelings against Taylor and "The Origins of the
Second World War" could be explained by his political
conservatism, Holland's proximity to Germany, his war
memories of Hitler, his suffering at the hands of the Germans (he was in Buchenwald for a year), and, above all,
perhaps, the different visions that Geyl and Taylor had
of the future. Taylor had pinpointed this very difference
in the conclusion of his Geyl panegyric. "Geyl speaks for
the Europe of the past as well as for the Europe of the
present," he had written. "He loves them both; and he
believes, as I do, that they present the highest point
which humanity has achieved. If his principles and
passions mislead him, it is, I think, more in relation
to the future than to the past. Loving the past so much,
he cannot believe that it will come to an end. He cannot believe that Europeans will cease to care for individual liberty and national diversity. I am not so sure.
It seems to me possible that men may come soon to
live only in the present; and that they will forget their
historical inheritance in favour of television sets and
washing machines. There will be no classes, no na-

tions, no religions; only a single humanity freed from labour by the electric current of atomic-power stations. European history will then be as dead as the history of ancient Egypt; interesting as a field of study but with nothing to say to us. . . . Our last conversation was just after the end of the Suez affair. I was jubilant. . . . National independence (of Egypt) had been vindicated; Anglo-French aggression had been defeated. Geyl was gloomy: he saw only the passing of European predominance. I think he was wrong. The Geyl of the twenty-first century may be an Indian or a Chinese — even perhaps an Egyptian. But maybe our light is going out. What matter? It has burnt with a noble flame."

To most Englishmen, whether philistine-barbarians or Hellenist-Hebraics, Taylor is not an unfamiliar figure, for his name appears in print with the regularity of the Sabbath or the scheduled television programs, and whether one's approach to culture is through newspapers (he appears in intellectual papers, like the *Observer*, the *Guardian*, the *New Statesman*, and in popular ones, like the Beaverbrook press), broadcasts (he often appears on television programs like "Brains Trust" and "Free Speech"), textbooks ("The Struggle for Mastery in Europe: 1848-1918"), a university (he is one of the three or four best lecturers at Oxford), or politics (he is a recalcitrant bow in the hair of the Labour Party, and a luminary of the Campaign for Nuclear Disarmament), Taylor inevitably turns out to be one of the main gate-

ways. At Magdalen, his Oxford college, where I had
dined two or three times, Taylor was often to be found
in the Senior Common Room at mealtimes on weekdays,
his glasses resting rather forbiddingly on his big nose as
he talked in a clipped, acid voice to half a dozen alter-
nately solemn and amused colleagues. He had a special
way with anecdotes, including a special way of smacking
his lips, often as a signal that he was about to tell an important story. As an undergraduate, I had sat in on some
of his lectures. They tended to be sliced into equal
halves, one meaty with the solid specificity of history and
the other juicy with histrionics, but among the undergraduates, always pressed for time, it was Taylor's use of his
day that was most marvelled at. It was said that he often
read and reviewed a book before breakfast, which he
took at eight o'clock. Then he worked steadily through
original documents (in five languages), with a break for
lunch, until late in the afternoon, when he met his tutees.
(He was patient and meticulous with clever pupils, impatient and hasty with the plodders.) He might finish off
his day by listening to music (for which he had a real
passion), by distributing his wit, like Dr. Johnson, among
his Oxford colleagues at the dinner table, or by talking,
like his hero John Bright, in a lecture hall in London.
Indeed, sometimes he spent half the week in London,
where he worked out of several libraries — at a little more
relaxed pace, it was hoped — and led the public life of a
prima donna. Even among those discriminating colleagues of his who deplored certain of his activities,

Taylor remained the subject of a sneaking admiration. One distinguished man of letters at Oxford, to whom comparisons and analogies, though hedged with qualifications, came as easily as daydreams come to most of us, had once summed Taylor up as "the Tolstoy of our time — um, with a difference," going on to explain, "Like Tolstoy, Taylor thinks the historical field of force is the microscopic facts, those millions of telegrams and dispatches, but while Tolstoy didn't think one could make sense of it — he was humble — Taylor thinks one can." The perversity of his responses to situations, which in undergraduate conversation was never far behind the mention of his name, was scarcely less a subject for wonder. One don recalled how he had found himself at a meeting of a Peace Congress behind the Iron Curtain and, glancing at the roster of speakers, had discovered Taylor's name there. "In the first place," he told me, with much relish, "it was astonishing that Taylor should be there at all — it was a very Party-line conference. Then, that he should be speaking! But the miracle was the speech he gave, to a dumb, stony house — it was dyed-in-the-wool conservative. And then he had the gall to come over to me and whisper in my ear, 'I've been dreaming of giving a speech like that since God knows when!' In Oxford, at a meeting of blue-blooded Conservatives, he would have delivered a stinging Left Wing harangue."

When I wrote to Taylor asking if he would talk about his view of history, he — unlike most other historians — made a perverse response. "I have no theories of history and I know nothing about them," he said. On reflection, this seemed more than contrary. He had written reviews dealing with practically all historical theoreticians, including Toynbee, Geyl, and Carr; he had been taken to task for his own theories of history by Trevor-Roper; and his lectures — indeed, his writings — many times turned out to be illustrations of his view that history is made up of accidents, with statesmen and politicians more often than not unable to control the events around them. But ultimately he agreed to talk to me at his suburban London house. I found Taylor in his living room one morning at eleven o'clock. He was wearing a mushroom-gray corduroy suit; his hair, which, though he is fifty-six, is abundant and only slightly gray, was neatly combed; and his glasses were forbidding as ever (he seemed to be peering at the world through a microscope), but the most noticeable thing about him was a permanent frown line — a sort of exclamation point — between the fierce circles of his eyes. Unlike Geyl's, the room was not inundated with historical works, though, as with Geyl, there was an impressive exhibit of books — they were displayed in a cabinet near a piano.

I said I understood he was "the real successor to Namier."

"I'm not sure I'd want to be his successor, though no one would deny his super gifts," he said, then added, "He took the mind out of politics, so I don't think he'll survive." The implication was that he himself did wish to survive. "Nobody would deny that Namier understood

Freud, but so do most professional journalists. Further-more, his attitude to psychoanalysis was more that of a patient than that of a psychoanalyst. It is thought that I was Namier's pupil. Strictly speaking, he was my pupil."

I said, "What do you mean?"

"During my eight-year spell at Manchester University, I instructed him in marking examination papers, in the hours of his lectures, and even in the subject matter of his classes," Taylor said. "For example, I used to send him little notes saying, 'You're meeting your class at such-and-such an hour, and it is a general, not an honors, class, so include *dates* in your lecture.' So you see, strictly speaking, he was my pupil in many things, though actual-ly he was a professor at the university and I was an as-sistant lecturer."

I had been told at Oxford that during Namier's life-time, Taylor had felt himself to be a little bit in his shadow. There was not a trace of his shadow in the room now, however; in fact, Taylor gave the impression of having come into his own quite early. His conversa-tion was tough and theatrical, and his small, pointed mouth had a way of snapping on words, like a rat trap. He talked as though he were seated at dinner in the Senior Common Room, with the assembled dons paying close attention to his words.

Treading gently, I approached his territory by asking him what Namier would have thought of "The Origins of the Second World War." (Although Trevor-Roper, in his review, had confidently asserted that the great historian would have squashed it, others had said, with equal assurance, that Namier would have saluted it.)

"He would probably have both liked it and not liked it," Taylor said wryly. "Take his 'Diplomatic Prelude.' It is distinctly a two-sided work. On the one hand, it recounts the mistakes of everybody. On the other hand, it reasserts Namier's lifelong anti-Germanism. My book *can* be read in two ways. In one way, it may sort of exonerate Hitler by saying the war was a mistake; in another, by letting Hitler off, it may make all Germans responsible for the war. Namier wouldn't have liked the implications about Hitler, but he might have been pleased by the anti-German implications."

Taylor was a beguiling man to talk with, partly because of his ability to turn everything one expected him to say topsy-turvy. "American critics were far cleverer than the English reviewers," he said now. "They declared the book to be bad because of its present-day implications: if all Germans are culpable for the war, then the present Western policy toward Germany is wrong. I have written that the First World War was a mistake, and I have written that the Second World War was a mistake."

He snapped his lips shut, and, for the first time, I felt the full political impact (as Trevor-Roper must have) of one sentence in the "Origins": "The war of 1939, far from being premeditated, was a mistake, the result on both sides of diplomatic blunders" — a sentence accurately described by the publisher on the book jacket as "shattering." If history was made up of "accidents," then there wasn't much hope for the future, for avoiding the Third World War. "Liking the book," Taylor said, "becomes a matter of politics. If you're a Left Winger and are against the bomb and the arming of Germany, you may be in sympathy with the thesis; if you're a conservative, a militarist, and for Germany in NATO, you may not be." Superficially, this seemed reasonable and free of paradoxical spikes, but on closer inspection it became something different; history seemed not only to be falling from the grace of objectivity to personal prejudices but to be slipping down into the abyss of political bias. Even if this could be explained on the ground of recent memories of the events under review, what followed couldn't be. "Obviously, historians like Sir John Wheeler-Bennett and Alan Bullock and the younger American practitioners are hostile to my book because, whether they know it or not, they have vested interests," Taylor was saying. "They have written textbooks, and they have their own books and legends to sell." It was difficult to tell whether or not Taylor was serious.

Now, however, he switched from the treacherous ground of *ad-hominem* argument to the safer one of evidence. "Until I started studying the records, I, like many of my reviewers, had swallowed the legends about pre-war history," he said. "I had accepted, for example — it's written in all the books — that Hitler sent for Schuschnigg. But when I looked into the records I discovered that it was the other way around — Schuschnigg asked to see Hitler." He seemed to be saying that small facts could change our picture of the past. "I was talking to Ian Gilmour, past editor of the *Spectator,* the other day," Taylor went on, smacking his lips, "who doesn't agree with my thesis. I told him two facts that, to say the least, surprised him. I told him that in the thirties the fate of the Jews in Poland was far worse than the fate of the Jews in Germany, and that in the thirties there were no extermination camps in Germany. Most people, like Ian, believe the reverse; prewar history is shrouded in legend. The records, however, just don't corroborate the legends. I wrote my history from the records. Ian and others *project* the later madness of Hitler back into the thirties. Without the carnage of the war, I wonder if he would have stumbled onto the idea of the gas chambers. In actual fact, even according to Bullock's 'Hitler,' which represents the orthodoxy, Hitler, avoiding the use of force, which would have been suicidal, became Chancellor and carried out the Nazi revolution by *legal, rational* means, and conducted his foreign policy shrewdly — no more madly, *insanely,* than any other statesman. According to the records, Hitler did his feeble best. Yes, he had his lunatic vision — and 'Mein Kampf' is a record of it — but he didn't behave like a lunatic all the time. I think all statesmen ought to be considered *first* on the basis of what they were trying to do, and what they did, according to the records. They ought to be taken as statesmen, as rational beings, before we resort to extraordinary, escapist, and easy explanations, like 'He was just insane.'" He again snapped shut his lips.

Some had traced the furor against the Hitler book to

Taylor's nihilist view of history ("a tale told by an idiot, full of sound and fury, signifying nothing"). If there were overtones of the "idiot" view in his notion of accident, his attempt to find a rationale for Germany's behavior muffled them. Now, like Namier, Taylor underrated the role of plans and ideas; now, unlike Namier, he found a "statesman," a man who had ideas and policies, even in Hitler. Moreover, while Namier might list the people who owed their jobs to, say, Thomas Pelham-Holles, Duke of Newcastle, the eighteenth-century politician, and note their tendencies to vote as a group in favor of Newcastle's policies (he stopped short of saying, "They voted with Newcastle *because* they owed their jobs to him." If there was even a hint of diagnosis — "X professes that he voted Whig principles, when actually he had no choice but to fall in line with his patron" — it was contained in bringing the true facts to the surface), Taylor, at least in the "Origins," subordinated his facts (how Hitler and Schuschnigg met, what the state of Jews in Germany was) to a thesis and to professed ideas and motives — of the dependent, say, in my Namier example, or of Hitler in his own book.

Taylor now turned to his critics, and impaled them on his quick wit. Beginning in a low key, he first dismissed Geyl in the terms one might have expected. "Geyl is too much of a moral historian," he said. "In his book on Napoleon, he roundly condemns him; I am not sure we should condemn him. Napoleon, like Hitler, went from stage to stage. Geyl thinks I ought to keep saying, again and again, 'Hitler was a wicked man.' I tend to think that once I have written a sentence about Hitler's wickedness I have dealt with the subject. Besides, Geyl has too many personal memories of Nazism." He stopped, as though he feared that he was saying something ordinary. He turned to Trevor-Roper, and up came the surprise-package side of Taylor's character again. "Hughie shouldn't have attacked me, because my views really agree with his," he said. "Not only did I agree with him when he attacked Toynbee and Carr — he wrote at length what most of us really thought, though he did go on a little too long, and also his 'Carr' came much too late — but we look at history in the same way. Unlike Hughie, I may be a determinist — I believe in large trends, like the continuous growth of German power before the First World War — but I always write very detailed studies, in which it is the accidents that seem to stick out and make up history. My books, therefore, really turn out to be illustrations of free will — to which Hughie attaches so much importance."

This was not only paradoxical but a little incomprehensible; the belief in "accidents" seemed to be a roundabout way to determinism, not to voluntarism. I wanted to clear up this theoretical confusion, but Taylor went straight on.

"The difference between Hughie and me may be no more than that of definition," he said. "If you regard a plan as a great vision, then, of course, Hitler did have a plan — a lunatic vision. But if you define 'plan' as I do, a plan of day-to-day moves, then Hitler didn't have one. In this connection, a review of my book that meant a great deal to me was written by a Cambridge historian, F. H. Hinsley. He defined 'plan' in yet another way. He said that while Hitler may not have had a pattern, the more he succeeded the more of a pattern he got; success became his pattern. This, I think, is a fruitful approach. But" — Taylor sighed, then stood up and started pacing the room — "Hughie's attack on me was full of misquotations and misreadings. Robert Kee, the moderator of our television debate, told me about Hughie's mistakes, and it was due to him that I looked into his article carefully and wrote my 'Exercises for Beginners.'"

Pausing in front of a shelf of his work, he took out of his collection "Englishmen and Others" (published five years before the Professor's *Encounter* attack), and brought it over to his chair. "I will read you something to show how much I admire Hughie," he said, looking through the book. "After I'd heard that Hughie was preparing an attack on the 'Origins,' the newspapers, by leaving out a 'not,' misquoted me on him." He was still looking for his passage. "What I really said was not 'It should be very amusing. He knows as much about twentieth-century history as I do about seventeenth-century history — which is to say nothing at all' but 'It should be very amusing. He knows as much about twentieth-century history as I do about seventeenth-century history — which is *not* to say nothing at all.'"

He laughed dryly, as though to say that journalism

wasn't what it should be, and then, in an unexpectedly tender voice, read his accolade to Trevor-Roper. It was no less generous than his appraisal of Geyl, and it struck me that, however he belied it (to many it could come as a surprise), Taylor was a historian with great warmth:

"No one cares now about Germany's bid to conquer Europe. Few care about the fate of Adolf Hitler. In the present situation of international politics both are better forgotten. Mr. Trevor-Roper's book ["The Last Days of Hitler"] would be forgotten along with them if it merely solved the riddle to which he was originally set. But it transcended its subject. Though it treated of evil men and degraded themes, it vindicated human reason. In a world where emotion has taken the place of judgment and where hysteria has become meritorious, Mr. Trevor-Roper has remained as cool and detached as any philosopher of the Enlightenment. Fools and lunatics may overrun the world; but later on, in some future century, a rational man will rediscover 'The Last Days of Hitler' and realize that there were men of his own sort still alive. He will wish, as every rational man must, that he had written Mr. Trevor-Roper's book. There are not many books in our age of which that could be said."

Resuming the subject of the controversy about the "Origins," he said, "The trouble with my book may be that in a number of places I left my own side very weak. I tend to think that if I have written one or two sentences about a theme, I repeat, that's the end of it, that's enough. In the first place, I know I know. In the second place, I know other people know; after all, I didn't write my book to be read as the only book on the origins of the Second World War. Now I am thinking of writing a long preface, when the storm has died down, in which I will answer my critics and point up some of the arguments for my case. Like the one about German armament: If Hitler had planned war in 1939, why weren't there more armament preparations in Germany?" Then he made the point that the future could add an element to the understanding of the past, and finished by saying, "I am a revisionist about the causes of the Second World War, but what would really embarrass me would be if someone like Harry Elmer Barnes, one of those raving American revisionists of the First World War, should like my book." (Within two months, Barnes was in print with a three-column letter to the New York *Times* extolling Taylor's book and attacking its reviewer in that paper.)

A boy of eleven or twelve, Taylor's son, sauntered in and, sitting down at the piano, ran through some scales. Over his shoulder, he informed me intensely that he was taking part in a neighborhood music festival that afternoon. He as much as turned us out of the room. We went outside into a small yard, at the edge of a quiet street, and, leaning over the hedge, Taylor talked a bit about himself. "I suppose"— he smacked his lips — "I am a sort of conventional radical from the north. I was educated in a Quaker school and then went to Oriel, Oxford — where I was the only member of the Labour Club in the college. I would have gone to Balliol if I hadn't messed up my examination."

In Oxford, there was a legend that Taylor, in applying

for entrance to Balliol, had done very well on his written papers but that at the interview, when he was asked what he planned to do after going down, he had characteristically replied, "Blow it up." Few, if any, of his interviewers at the serious college had cracked a smile; they had just kept the would-be *pétroleur* out. I asked Taylor if the story had a basis in fact. He chuckled, and replied, "If it does, I said, 'Oxford *should* be blown up.'" He sighed (sighing was one of his many histrionic mannerisms, as dramatic as his phrasing), and said, "Now I have a vested interest in Oxford and I don't think it ought to be blown up quite yet — not till I am retired. [Sometime later, Taylor created a flurry in the newspapers by threatening to leave Oxford if his special lectureship — gravy from the university for senior dons — were terminated, as the regulations required.] I like living in Oxford. I like the surroundings, the life. But by no means am I as happy at Oxford as I was in noisy, industrial Manchester." The ordinary attitude, of course, would have been the reverse. He went on in the same vein. "The countryside around Manchester is much more pleasant than the countryside around Oxford. Besides, I was young and had young friends, and we used to go out of the city three or four days a week and have a lot of fun. The other thing besides my radicalism that shows through my writing of history is my northernness. You see, in the north people are much tougher; in the south they are more traditional, conservative — soft."

I mentioned his journalistic activities, and got an unexpected response.

"I don't know whether I am more a professional journalist or a historian," he said, and, perhaps realizing from my expression that I thought this a strange remark for one of the leading English historians to make, he said something even stranger. "If you look at my income, you will find I get more money out of journalism than I do out of history."

I asked him what he meant by "a professional journalist."

"A professional journalist is he who pleases his editor," Taylor said. He seemed to delight in my puzzlement. "I think the *Sunday Express* [most educated Englishmen consider it a rag] is a much better paper — I have a contract with it — than the *Times*. The *Times* is softheaded. When you see the causes they have sponsored in the past, you can't help coming out on the side of the *Sunday Express*." All of a sudden, he made a concession to my growing bewilderment. "It is only fair to say," he added, pinching his nose, "that I was brought up in the Manchester *Guardian* tradition. We didn't take to the *Times* at all."

He turned to a discussion of his methods of writing. "I try not to write more than a thousand words a day. This is a negative principle, as I do not positively write a thousand words a day; it's just that I won't write anything more than that. Since I am writing for the papers all the time — besides teaching, though never

more than ten hours a week — I never get more than
two or three thousand words done on a book in a week.
Much of my past work thus far I have written from
intellectual capital, stored up from my earlier researches,
but the book I am working on now is quite another
matter." It was a major work for the fifteen-volume
"The Oxford History of England" from Roman Britain
to the present, he told me, and was to cover English
history from 1914 to 1945. "Also," he went on, "some of
my time is taken up with just getting hold of the books
I need. I am not a book hoarder; I work out of the
libraries, and although at Oxford I can get to books
quite easily, the closest library here is about five miles
away. But I am fast on the typewriter."

A car started somewhere down the street, and Taylor
stopped talking until it had passed. I asked him whether
he had been to America.

"Yes and no," he answered. "I went across to Canada
— to New Brunswick, to get an honorary degree — and
then I did look America full in the face. I leaned over"
— he bent forward —"and had a good look at the hills
of Maine. So in a way I have been and not been."

I asked him if he had a wish to visit America.

"I don't think so," he said. "I have two interests. One
is buildings, and America doesn't have any buildings —
I mean old buildings, like cathedrals. The other interest
is food and wine. From my little experience of Canada,
the Americans have neither good food nor good drink.
In this interest I am an unconventional radical. You

see, I have been corrupted by the good life; I now find even living in industrial cities depressing. I imagine, as societies, America and Russia have a lot in common."

"What do you think of Russia?" I asked.   .

"I think it's heading toward good," he said, "though Communism, like Catholicism, is by now top-heavy."

As a parting shot, I risked a question that had been itching at the back of my mind. I asked Taylor if his use of paradoxes in speech and in writing had any purpose behind it.

"I am not at all paradoxical," he said, brushing aside all the paradoxes of our conversation, not to mention the innumerable paradoxical sentences in his works. "The reason people think I am paradoxical, if they do think that, is that I have a clear and sharp style. And I can't see that there is any harm in having a clear and sharp style."

We went into the house, so that Taylor could ring for a taxi — his son was playing a vigorous waltz, but Taylor managed to make himself heard over the music — and then returned to the yard. As I was getting into the taxi, Taylor said, "After you have lived with books as long as I have, you start preferring them to people." That seemed to be a parting jab at me. Before the taxi pulled away, he was laughing.

As I sat in my room, the opening of the "profile" of Taylor that had appeared in the *Observer* following the publication of the "Origins"— perhaps the best single short piece ever written on the mercurial man — came

back to me. The lines were unattributed, but they had
the look of J. Douglas Pringle, an excellent leader writer
and a close friend of both Namier and Taylor. "In the
eighteenth century," the phrases rang out, "dons were
indolent, obscure men who drank themselves to sleep
each night with port and claret. In the nineteenth
century, they were austere, dedicated scholars, still
celibate, often eccentric, whose only concession to the
hurly-burly of life outside their college walls was an
occasional review, vitriolic but anonymous, in the *Edin-
burgh Quarterly*. In the twentieth century, they advise
governments, sit on Royal Commissions, fight elections,
marry — and remarry — produce plays, write detective
stories, and entertain us on the telly. None of them has
enjoyed this minor revolution more than A. J. P. Taylor. . . ." Yet from under the deft ink Taylor emerged,
as always, a jack-in-the-box. I now tried to put him
together, but, like many before me, I simply saw the
serious historian, the Manchester radical, the tutor, the
journalist, the *bon vivant*, and the lover of music —
all of them equally real. What Taylor undoubtedly
achieved, often with unsurpassed brilliance, he seemed
to mar with his antics, and for me the proportion of
mischief to intelligence in his last and most controversial book remained a puzzle. There was, for example,
an ambiguous passage in the "Origins" in which Taylor
both defended his case and almost willfully delivered
himself into the hands of his critics:

Hitler was an extraordinary man. . . . But his policy is

capable of rational explanation; and it is on these that history is built. The escape into irrationality is no doubt easier. The blame for war can be put on Hitler's Nihilism instead of on the faults and failures of European statesmen — faults and failures which their public shared. Human blunders, however, usually do more to shape history than human wickedness. At any rate, *this is a rival dogma which is worth developing, if only as an academic exercise* [my italics].

Once, during a lecture, I had heard Taylor say, "Error can often be fertile, but perfection is always sterile," and it seemed to me, upon a second reading of the "Origins," that this remark, if anything, might be the key to Taylor's book.

Both Taylor and Geyl, in their different ways, had argued that history was a debate. But if history was an argument or an academic exercise, could we *ever* discover what really happened? What was the truth about the past? How could we tell? If both Taylor and Geyl could be wrong, *who* could be right? Carr seemed to think that in his book "What Is History?" he had dealt with these and countless other historiographical questions. "In some respects," the reviewer in the *Times Literary Supplement* had said of the book, "it is the best statement of its kind ever produced by a British historian." The reviewer noted, "Much though Mr. Carr has absorbed from the Marxist conception of history, he does not identify himself with it and maintains a certain reserve towards it; and in spite of his explicit criticisms of the British tradition, especially of its empiricist strand, he is of it, even if not quite in it. Indeed, he picks up the threads of British philosophy of history where R. G. Collingwood left them about a quarter of a century ago. . . . If he does not bring to his job Collingwood's philosophical sense and subtlety, he is greatly superior to his predecessor as both historian and political theorist."

I found Carr, who is seventy, in the living room of his Cambridge house. The room was lined with bookshelves, but they bulged with manila folders, and there wasn't a book in the room. Carr appeared to be a historian who, like Taylor, worked out of libraries. When I entered, Carr was reposing on an enormous brown sofa. His feet were bare, and there was a pair of rope-soled sandals on the floor beside him, suggesting that sandals were his regular footwear. He stood up to greet me. He was a hulking man, with white hair. His face was rather hawklike, and tapered from a prominent forehead to a pointed but also prominent chin. He was dressed in baggy, donnish trousers, an old gray-and-white tweed jacket, and a well-worn necktie. Having drawn up a chair for me next to his sofa, he lay back as before, the picture of a don, who has as little use for appearances and possessions and the other accoutrements of living as a high priest.

"To study the historian before his history, what in your background, would you say, explains your set of ideas?" I asked, borrowing a leaf from his book.

"Well, now"— his voice was as warm and comforting as eider down —"I grew up in a rather suburban atmosphere in North London, in a closed society of forty or fifty relatives. I went to day school and then to Trinity, Cambridge, which I chose because it was the *largest* and the *best* college in the university." After Cambridge, he continued, he had spent twenty years with the Foreign Office: in Riga, where he taught himself Russian; in Paris, where he improved his French; and in London, where he learned the proper use and importance of diplomatic documents and wrote a book on Dostoevski and one on Herzen and his circle. Then he left the Foreign Office to write history, and to take a chair at the University College of Wales, in Aberystwyth. On the way to being appointed a research fellow at his old college — his present position — he'd also written leaders for the London *Times* and taught at Balliol. "When I was younger," he said, "I found stimulation in teaching young minds, but now it would simply bore me. I have always been rather restless and on the move. Intellectually, like Toynbee — and perhaps Isaiah Berlin, too — I belonged to the pre-1914 liberal tradition, which had as its credo a belief in rational progress, a progress through compromise, and in History with a capital letter. Since 1914, all of us, in one way or another, have been reacting against our liberal environment — I have spent much of my time studying the Russian Revolution, which hardly represents a progress through compromise — but the faith in some sort of progress

still clings to me, and is really the main issue between
Berlin and Trevor-Roper and their followers, on one
side, and me, on the other. I see the Golden Age
looming ahead of us; Berlin probably sees it behind us,
in the nineteenth century; Trevor-Roper may still be
searching for it somewhere in the past — he hasn't
written enough to give himself away even on that."

I asked him what he thought of his critics.

"It's not very difficult to answer them, or their self-
appointed spokesman, Trevor-Roper," he said. "Actually, I feel insulted that he let me off so lightly. I
thought I was at least as great a villain as Toynbee or
Taylor. Why do you suppose Trevor-Roper didn't see
me for what I really am?"

He exuded good cheer. If he seemed invulnerable,
it was not because he was spiky or wore battle dress or
talked against a thunderous background of battalions
but because he came across as a sort of Greek god —
one who might have many human failings but nevertheless *was* a god.

"My critics, on the whole," he said, raising himself a
little on his sofa and wiggling his toes, "simply repeat
the old charges that have been ringing in my ears for
many years." They had said that for Carr history was
a power and success story, and was not objective. He
was a complete relativist. They carped. What about
those failed men in history? What about the great
Western tradition of trying always to know the facts?
What about conservative and radical historians flower-

ing in the same cultural milieu? "I've always said," Carr continued, answering them now, "that nobody can write about the winners without writing about the losers, without going over, step by step, the whole conflict — the entire game. About those facts — for me history is a river, and you cannot step in the same river twice. By history as a river, I mean that you can never have a twentieth-century Mozart; you may have a genius comparable to Mozart, but the musical idiom and style today are so different from those of the eighteenth century that a new Mozart would have to compose in a radically different way. And, finally, different types of historians, people with different shades of opinion, can emerge from the same society because of personal factors — their home environment, school and college, and so on."

I put myself in the place of his critics, and pressed him on a couple of points of this debate with his detractors. I said that if, according to his theory, the losers had a role in history that was equivalent to the role of the winners, why hadn't he given them more than a few pages in his six-volume "A History of Soviet Russia"?

"That is the fault of my 'History,' not of my theory of history," he replied. (Isaac Deutscher, a distinguished biographer of our times — he shared Carr's theory of conflict — had given space to the programs and aspirations of practically every splinter group when writing his book on Trotsky, "The Prophet Unarmed.")

I took up another point. "When people complain that

your theory would lead the historian to be cavalier with facts, aren't they saying more than you suppose?" I asked. "Aren't they saying that the function of a historian is to reconstruct, in all its complexity, what really happened? Aren't they saying that a historian should study fifth-century Athens for its own sake, rather than as just another link in the chain of history? You would have them study fifth-century Greece in relation to the importance it had for the fourth or third century B.C., or, indeed, the twentieth century A.D. Isn't there more value in *objectivity* — in trying to put ourselves, as far as possible, in the sandals of, say, a fifth-century Greek statesman and to view the landscape of problems as he did, considering the alternatives he had before his eyes when he made a particular decision?"

"Yes," he said. "This is the heart of the attack. But in my view it's not possible to study a period on its own, in isolation from what happened before and after it. History is a process, and you cannot isolate a bit of process and study it on its own. My theory is that the facts of the past are simply what human minds make of them, and what these minds make of them depends on the minds' place in the movement."

If one accepted Carr's contention that history was movement, a process, a river, *if* one accepted his "faith in the future of society and in the future of history," I thought, then his conclusions did seem more or less irresistible. "But isn't your faith perhaps naïve, incapable of logical proof?" I asked.

"Yes, it is," he said. "But then every faith is naïve. Faith is something you cannot prove. You just believe it. Actually, all those theoretical differences are really a smoke screen for the real difference between my critics and me. As I said before, basically we are just at odds about the position of the Golden Age."

"I got the impression from the rejoinder in the *Listener* to your attack on Berlin — your most persuasive critic — that the crux of your disagreement was determinism," I said.

"If it is determinism to think that men are a product of their society, that their actions are conditioned by the society, then, as opposed to Berlin, I am a determinist," Carr said. "You see, I don't think there are such things as bad people. To us, Hitler, at the moment, seems a bad man, but will they think Hitler a bad man in a hundred years' time or will they think the German *society* of the thirties bad?"

"But the very fact that you aren't prepared to call people bad but are prepared to call *things* bad," I said, "shows that you are prejudiced against free will, that you have a bias in favor of putting the blame on things, on society, on environment."

"Yes, that's perfectly true," he said. "I think people are the result of their environment. Berlin thinks that because I don't believe each individual can modify the course of history, in some bad sense of the word I am a determinist. But if I say that without peasants there wouldn't have been any revolution, am I not saying something about the individual peasant — for what are peasants if not a collection of individuals? I don't deny the individual a role, I only give society a role equal to that of the individual. The reason all this rings as determinism in Berlin's ears, I insist, is that he tends to regard history as a succession of accidents; otherwise, why would he begin his 'Historical Inevitability' with a Bernard Berenson quotation?"

Berlin had opened his lecture with the following passage: "Writing some ten years ago in his place of refuge during the German occupation of Northern Italy, Mr. Bernard Berenson set down his thoughts on what he called the 'accidental view of History': 'It led me,' he declared, 'far from the doctrine lapped up in my youth about the inevitability of events and the Moloch still devouring us today, "historical inevitability." I believe less and less in these more than doubtful and certainly dangerous dogmas, which tend to make us accept whatever happens as irresistible and foolhardy to oppose.'"

"I have read Berenson's 'The Accidental View of History,'" Carr continued, lying back on his sofa, "and I think the natural consequence of his accidental view is that events are causeless — you can't say, for instance, that the depression caused Hitler."

That Berlin had begun "Historical Inevitability" with a Berenson remark was not sufficient evidence for me that he accepted Berenson's views on accidents. Indeed, in his rebuttal to Carr, Berlin had proved — to me, at least — that he believed events did have causes. "I think that in your book you misinterpret Berlin and Popper," I said. "When you say they don't believe in causes, I don't think that's quite fair. For example, what you call causes Popper, in his books, calls 'logic of situation,' and he and Berlin certainly believe in it. If they didn't believe that historians should study causes, they would have to believe in abolishing the study of history. It seems to me that the basic difference between you and your opponents is that you tend to take a much more sociological view of history; they don't see everything as a manifestation of an omnipotent society."

"I can't see a possible alternative to my sociological view of history," he said. "It seems to me that everything is completely interconnected. If I did misread some of these people a little, you must remember that I wasn't writing a treatise — I was writing lectures. Also," he added, "I love writing polemics and love reading good polemics. That's why I was disappointed in Trevor-Roper's 'Success Story' — because it was a bad polemic."

Carr got up from the sofa and slipped his feet into the rope-soled sandals. "I'll ask my wife for some tea," he said, and walked toward the door.

The Flight of Crook-Taloned Birds

METAPHYSICALLY inclined thinkers, like Marx, Spengler, and Toynbee (plum-cake historians), have
had a large, all-embracing explanation of history — why
things happen as they do — which they demonstrate
with a nod now and again to examples. The professional
academics (dry-biscuit historians), like R. H. Tawney
and Sir Lewis Namier, respectively, detect causal connections between religion and capitalism, or between
Parliament and the self-interest of the M.P.s, or, like
Taylor, notice a discrepancy between an intention and
an action, and then arrive at small theories — why
particular things happen at a particular time — which
they substantiate with analysis, illustrate with exhaustive examples, or prove, however obliquely or indirectly, by a sustained narrative of events. Miss C. V.
Wedgwood belongs to neither of these schools. She is
a shortbread historian. She tells stories simply and en-
tertainingly, in the manner of Somerset Maugham (that

is, without the deep psychological perceptions of Proust, the sensitive nerve ends of James, or the linguistic virtuosity of Joyce; the historian counterparts of these literary figures almost always come out of one or the other of the two schools), or as the Victorian Carlyle or Edwardian G. M. Trevelyan did — straight, and with an unerring eye for the dramatic. Like Carlyle and Trevelyan, Miss Wedgwood seldom, if ever, fishes in the treacherous waters of philosophy or psychology. Because she has no theories to prove, her histories generously give the available facts a hearing, without rigorously applying the aristocratic principles of exclusion and selection, and if her democratic approach toward facts crowds her narrative as densely as the mainland of China, the terrain of her history, unlike the mainland of China, is seldom overrun by a mob; her felicity of style and mastery of the language for the most part keep the mob at bay, and carry the brimming narrative forward like a mountain stream. Miss Wedgwood, however, has felt the need to justify her nineteenth-century approach to history by once in a while delivering a theoretical pronouncement. She wrote, in a book of essays called "Truth and Opinion":

My writing experience has led me to set a very high value on investigating *what* men did and *how* things happened. Pieces like "The Last Masque" and "Captain Hind the Highwayman" [the first about Charles I, the second about one of his supporters] were written partly to provide entertainment; they are small literary diversions. But they were also written because limited and relatively simple subjects like these, where passion and prejudices play little part, give the historian an opportunity for the purest kind of enquiry. The apparent objectives may seem light and even frivolous, but the experiment in reconstructing as accurately and fully as possible a detached incident or a character *without attempting to prove any general point or demonstrate any theory whatsoever* is a useful exercise. I have found by experience that in the course of such neutral enquiries unexpected clues are found to far more important matters. "The Last Masque" gave me numerous indications for lines of enquiry into the Court and administration of Charles I and "Captain Hind" has left me with a handful of hints, ideas, and sources for the social consequences of the Civil War. The older historians concentrated more on narrative than on analysis, on the *How* rather than the *Why* of history. But now, for several generations, *Why* has been regarded as a more important question than *How*. It is, of course, a more important question. But it cannot be answered until *How* is established. The careful, thorough, and accurate answer to the question *How* should take the historian a long way towards answering the question *Why;* but for this purpose narrative history must be written with depth and reflection.

Miss Wedgwood's detractors in both the plum-cake and the dry-biscuit schools might retort — indeed, they often do — that narrative history is the least neglected aspect of history; that the *How* is much more easily apprehended than the *Why;* that the *How* does not advance knowledge, does not develop new variations on old explanations, does not introduce new ways of thinking about old facts; and that the life of a *How* history is scarcely as long as that of a fashion in ladies' hats, since no sooner has a researcher turned up a handful of new facts than the narrative is dated and a new one has to be constructed. But Miss Wedgwood's detractors realize that she is aware of all this, and they also realize that their objections and her defense are beside the point, for her natural gifts are unanalytical and literary, and she can no more resist writing narrative history than they can help writing metaphysical or academic history. Ever since I had first read her books some years before, I'd wanted to meet her, perhaps as much as anything because of her fine prose and her uncontainable interest in history. "By the time I was twelve," she had written in one of her essays collected in "Velvet Studies," published some fifteen years ago, "my writing had grown dangerously swift. There was a special kind of writing pad called 'The Mammoth,' two hundred pages, quarto, ruled faint; under my now practiced pen Mammoths disappeared in a twinkling. 'You should write history,' my father said, hoping to put on a brake. 'Even a bad writer may be a useful historian.' It was damping, but it was sense. It was, after all, unlikely that I would ever be Shakespeare."

To learn more about Miss Wedgwood and her *How* history, I now invited her to lunch with me in London — at Plato's, a quiet Greek restaurant whose glass front looks out on Wigmore Street. I waited for her at a small table near the glass wall. She arrived a little late, and grasped my hand warmly. Without any further formalities, she seated herself across from me and started talking ebulliently, as though we had known each other for years.

"I am sorry not to be prompt, but right across the street I discovered a Wedgwood china shop," she said. "For the family's sake, I had to look in the window — the Wedgwoods have been in the china business ever since the eighteenth century — although, being a seventeenth-century historian, I don't know much about the history of Wedgwood china." Miss Wedgwood, who is fifty-two, gray-haired, and brown-eyed, was conservatively and tastefully dressed in an English-cut suit. She spoke in an effervescent voice. "My interest in history is a very long one," she continued. "My father, not being the eldest son — here I go off on a tangent, my Achilles' heel — instead of going into the family china business, went into railways, so when I was a girl we did a lot of hard and bouncy travelling in Europe. In railways, as in the china business, there is a sort of freemasonry of the trade, and we had as many free passages as we wanted."

Miss Wedgwood paused for the first time, and I asked her if she would like a drink. She ordered a dry vermouth on ice, and went on talking. "When I was a girl — here I go off on a tangent again — I went to a day school in Kensington, from which everybody moved on to a proper, high-powered school, like St. Paul's Girls' School, but I liked it so much there that I stayed on. So few of us stayed back that we were given what amounted to private tuition. When I was fifteen, I finished, and thereupon immediately rushed off to Germany to live with a family and learn German. I rushed back to England to take the Scholarship examination for Lady Margaret Hall, Oxford, and rushed off again, this time to a family in France, to learn French." She stirred her vermouth.

"Would you like to order?" I asked.

"Oh, I almost forgot," she said. She studied the menu and ordered egg-and-lemon soup, moussaka, and a glass of red wine, and went on talking. "When I came down from Oxford," she said, "I decided I'd do a thesis with Tawney on some forbidding seventeenth-century subject. Had I gone on with it, I would have become a *Why* historian, but I didn't. I discovered that in *Why* history research is much more important than writing, and I wanted to do both. I really decided to become a *How* historian when, a little later, my father arranged for me to go and spend a weekend at the house of Trevelyan, who was then fifty-five; my father, Trevelyan, G. E. Moore, and Ralph Vaughan Williams had all been at Cambridge together and knew each other very well. Trevelyan was a great *How* historian, and he encouraged me to write a biography of the Earl of Strafford, which I did, instead of doing my thesis with Tawney. The biography was very feminine and sentimental. Sir John Neale, who writes two kinds of history — the literary and the analytic — with equal success, helped me to revise it and place it with a publisher. Ever since then, I have been writing *How* history continuously. I am not embarrassed to say that I write about the surface things — men in action, how the decisions were taken on the spot. I don't have much patience with secondary sources, which stud the *Why* historians' pages in the form of bulky footnotes."

I recalled that she had once written:

Whether it is that I have never quite outgrown the first excitement of that discovery [reading Pepys, Clarendon, and Verney when she was just a girl], I find in myself to this day an unwillingness to read the secondary authorities which I have difficulty in overcoming. Indeed it is rather the fear of some learned reviewer's "the author appears to be ignorant of the important conclusions drawn by Dr. Stumpfnadel" than a desire to know those conclusions for their own sake which, at the latter end of my own researches, drives me to consult the later authorities.

Miss Wedgwood was by now in the middle of her egg-and-lemon soup. "The *Why* historians," she said, "start with the assumption that there are deep-seated motives and reasons for most decisions, and they concentrate on that rather than on the action. Sometimes, happily for me, the historical characters surprise their *Why* historians by, say, not voting in a Parliament in accordance with their party and economic interests, as they should have voted. But this sort of thing doesn't seem to have daunted the *Why* historians very much, for the general preoccupation in this country and century remains *Why* history; in our universities the *How* history has mostly gone by the board." Countless historians had investigated the causes of the English Civil War, she went on, but they had been so mesmerized by the *Why* of the Civil War that, reading them, one would never know that England in that time had a day-to-day foreign policy. Indeed, in Miss Wedgwood's opinion, they themselves often forgot it, and were misled in their analyses. They enriched history by delving into its undercurrents, but they impoverished it by not gathering all its froth into their pages. "I know that many good historians are intolerant of my way of doing history," Miss Wedgwood said, putting her soupspoon down. "They say it's popular and short-lived. In a sense, I agree with them. Does that surprise you?"

"No," I said. (I had read in her "Velvet Studies": "At twelve I had no theory of history. Since then I have had many, even for some years the theory that in the interests of scholarship it is wrong to write history comprehensible to the ordinary reader, since all history so written must necessarily be modified and therefore incorrect. This was I think always too much against my nature to have held me long.")

"Women are very sensitive and self-conscious about what is said about them," she went on. "I think the mansion of history has enough rooms to accommodate all of us. I mean many sorts of history can be illuminating — and by 'illuminating' I mean you can show things by the way you relate them. When I was young, I was Left Wing and intolerant, prepared to damn many books and many ways of doing things. Now that I am a little older, I can tolerate many points of view and many types of books."

Over her moussaka, Miss Wedgwood told me that she had lived in London ever since she came down from Oxford, and had made ends meet by writing successful history books, by reviewing, by "being on every prize committee," and by doing a lot of work for the B.B.C.

I asked her if she had ever felt the lack of a university connection and a secure income.

"I haven't, because I really can't teach," she said. "Once, I did teach for a bit, and found that most of the pupils I thought were brilliant failed their examinations." She laughed.

The waiter brought her a cup of coffee, and also a Turkish delight, which she unwrapped slowly and carefully, as though she were peeling an orange. "By temperament, I am an optimist," she said. "But I am very gloomy about the uses and lessons of history. The whole study at times seems to me useless and futile. I give lectures now and again about the uses of history, but I always come home with a sinking feeling of whistling in the dark."

If history were simply a series of rough guesses, more art than science, as narrative historians from Thomas Babington Macaulay to Trevelyan, Miss Wedgwood's mentor, have thought, Miss Wedgwood would have even more claim to our attention than she now has. But ours is an age of analysis, of science, and at least for the moment fireside historians are flickering under the cold gust of the "why"s. Many historians may disagree with Miss Wedgwood that history is whistling in the dark, but few have the resources to light up the shadowy mansion of history. Two of them in our time who appear to have had batteries and torches strong enough for the illumination are R. H. Tawney, 1880-1962, and Sir Lewis Namier, 1888-1960 — both *Why* historians.

To learn something about Tawney and Namier and their *Why* histories, I thought it would be pleasant as well as useful to take up residence at Balliol, the old college of both of them, and perhaps talk history with my tutors, with whom I had studied the subject (the nontheoretical variety) for three years. But when I went up to Oxford, I found that Balliol, which had survived for six hundred and ninety-nine years (preparations were then under way to celebrate the seven-hundredth anniversary), had altered beyond my expectations, even though, as these things went, I was a recent graduate. Walking through the quadrangles, I sensed that a great gulf divided me from the people around me. In the few years since I had gone down, a new body of undergraduates had entered the shell of the college. In the desert of new Balliol faces, however, there was one familiar landmark, the tall figure of my close friend Jasper Griffin. He and I had come up to the college in the same year, and had found ourselves living next door to each other; indeed, in the affluent days of the college, our two rooms had formed a suite, and among its occupants had been Gerard Manley

Hopkins. It was discovering that Hopkins was a favorite of both of us that had drawn us together and begun our long friendship. As it happened, when the college elected him to a Junior Fellowship in Classics, he was given my old room as his office. Since he now lived out of college and worked mostly in the libraries, he let me have my old room back for the duration of my stay at Oxford. The room was intact, but again, like the student body, the staff of Balliol historians had changed. A. B. Rodger, who had brought me to love the manicured English countryside of the eighteenth century, had died. R. W. Southern, one of the greatest living English medievalists, who had led me to the springs of Anglo-Saxon and medieval history very much like a soldier leading a recalcitrant horse to water, had since been raised to a chair connected with another college. Even my external tutor, James Joll — he had conducted me through the tortuous European politics terminating in the First and Second World Wars — was at Harvard for a few months. Of the tutors who had tended me term after term, Christopher Hill, an authority on sixteenth- and seventeenth-century history, was one of the two or three still at the college. Like Southern, he was in high feather; he was holding the post of Ford's Lecturer, a distinguished university appointment, for the year. In several quarters he was regarded as the spiritual heir of Tawney, who in some ways had personified the traditions of Balliol, which to its adulators is "the best teaching college in the world" (the Oxford tutorial system is thought to have originated there) and to its detractors is a mere "teaching shop." Like Tawney, Hill had spent much of his life studying and teaching the history of the Puritans and of the birth of revolutionary ideas and ideals in seventeenth-century England. It was no surprise to me, therefore, that when I saw Hill, who is fifty — his three hallmarks are a legendary shyness, pithy sentences, and high, bouncy black hair — in his college room we conversed about Balliol, about teaching, about the English historical scene, and about Tawney.

As Hill talked, I couldn't help feeling that some of his observations on Tawney were applicable to himself. At one point, he said, "Tawney thought, and I agree, that anyone can write narrative histories, but that it is the analytic histories that advance knowledge. Of course, both Namier and Tawney were analytical historians, but they had very different spiritual fathers; it is impossible to conceive of Namier without Freud or of Tawney without Marx — Marx because the main feature of Tawney's work is a never-failing concern for the underdog in history. Namier's contribution was to go below the surface of public records to private papers and diaries, and Tawney's great contribution was asking the right questions. Surely part of good history is to *ask* the right questions. By *right* questions, I mean those that produce fruitful answers. Indeed, once he is supposed to have said, 'What historians need is not more documents but stronger boots.' Whereas Namier only recorded facts and left you to draw your own conclusions, Tawney put forward tremendously interesting hypotheses, which were not considered in the old, established histories, though these were often more accurate and learned than Tawney's. You remember going through with me those dozens of volumes on the Puritan Revolution by S. R. Gardiner and C. H. Firth? Well, those incomparably learned Victorians took it for granted, until Tawney, that the seventeenth-century English Parliament represented the *people*. Nor did they distinguish between different social classes; they wrote as though the Puritan Revolution were a struggle for liberty by *all* the people and *all* the classes. No historian thinks of the Puritan Revolution in those terms now, and it's all due to Tawney and his questions. In some ways, of course, Tawney was traditional and Victorian. For him, as for his Victorian counterparts, knowledge and virtue were one. Indeed, he used his researches to carry through reforms in society. Unlike the Victorians, however, he studied social and economic history. He directed the gaze of historians away from the narrow stage of politics and action to the infinitely wider one of society and life, opening up vast territories of interest and evidence for them to tend and reap. But perhaps his greatest achievement was discovering and developing the connections, in England, between religion and the rise of capitalism. One thing that made Tawney great in my eyes was his politics. He was a deeply committed Christian Socialist. His Christianity was very much akin to Sandy Lindsay's [former master of Balliol, A. D. Lindsay] and to Oliver Cromwell's —'Trust in God and keep your powder dry.' Heavenly intervention went hand in hand with human action. Tawney's Socialism wasn't the state variety — state ownership of industries, and so on — but a very individual sort of Socialism. Here again he was kin to Sandy Lindsay. Where he got his Christian Socialism I don't know — probably not at Rugby, his public school. Perhaps at Balliol. The Balliol of the early nineteen-hundreds, his time, was far more Left Wing and radical than that of the nineteen-sixties. Another thing that perhaps made him great was his lifelong work for the Workers' Educational Association, or W.E.A. He gave up a Balliol fellowship to continue in adult education, and accepted his professorship at the London School of Economics quite late in life. Still another thing that made him great was his combination of shrewdness and gentleness. He was a very shrewd man — he could see through people — but he never took issue with anyone on personal matters, always on principles."

After talking to Hill, I spent a little time in our college library, reading books and articles both by and about Tawney, whose name is a byword for the Tudor period. Going through the Tawney shelf made me remember my first essay, which had been written with the aid of Tawney's books, some of them forty years old. My assignment was "What, If Anything, Can Be Salvaged, About the Gentry and the Causes of the English Civil War, from the 'Gentry Controversy'?" It called for reading and evaluating one of Tawney's most famous theses. Tawney maintained that the moneyed classes, or the gentry, of the sixteenth and seventeenth centuries had risen on "the crushed bodies of the peasants" and on the debts owed them by the wasteful and dissipated hereditary class, causing the Civil War. By the use of better agricultural techniques and economic ruthlessness, the gentry had acquired land (it was the symbol of status) and money, but they had not acquired power, which, instead of accompanying the gentry's acquisition of land, had remained in the grasp of the Crown and the nobility, opening a political chasm. As soon as the gentry discovered that war was a cheaper means than litigation of wresting land and power from the wellborn bankrupt, they struck, setting England adrift in the waters of revolution. Trevor-Roper, in a thunderous charge, had long since cut through this view, yet in Tawney's history there remained such a store of research and wisdom that every new start on the causes of the Civil War began with him. Perhaps the reason was that while, with each wave of new evidence, the narrative historians were superseded (since the great excavations of the nineteenth and twentieth centuries, even the narrative hunks in the third volume of Gibbon's "Decline and Fall" retained only a literary interest), the analytic, the interpretive historians had a touch of immortality about them. (About evidence, the stuff of *How* history, Tawney had once written, "The first feeling of a person who sees a manuscript collection such as that at Holkham must be 'If fifty maids with fifty mops —,' and a sad consciousness that the mop which he wields is a very feeble one.") Even though his examples were dated, many of his statistics revised, and (sometimes under the impetus of his own ideas and researches) his theses jettisoned, we undergraduates yet turned to his histories for their functional value as works of understanding.

During his long career, which spanned more than fifty years, he wrote two kinds of works — historical and Socialist. His histories, such as "The Agrarian Problem in the Sixteenth Century" (marked by social morality: faith in the potentiality of ordinary men and distrust of the arrogance of the rich and the powerful — equalled only by his distaste for the specialist), created a minor revolution, making possible a new kind of history, with new actors. In his histories, he presented, in powerful Elizabethan prose, the state of Tudor society, letting the yeoman, the peasant, the displaced farmer speak — in many cases for the first time; in his Socialist books, such as "The Acquisitive Society" and "Equality," he drew aside the veil of hypocrisy, exposing the discrepancy between the Christian ethic and the actual condition of modern society. The late Hugh Gaitskell said of these works, "[They] made a tremendous impact upon my generation. . . . If you ask me why we were so impressed, I think it was really . . . that these books combined passion and learning. There was nothing false or exaggerated in them. . . . He was not inventing things but simply showing them to us — things we had failed to appreciate before but which we recognized immediately he wrote about them." As a political thinker, Tawney became the social conscience of his age. Indeed, Sidney and Beatrice Webb thought that he was destined to be a Labour Prime Minister of England — an ambition that many nursed for him but that was made impossible by poor health resulting from wounds he received in the First World War. (He himself didn't set much store by honors; when Sidney Webb and he were offered peerages by the Ramsay MacDonald government, Webb accepted and he declined.) With the improvement in the condition of the working classes and the beginning of the welfare era in England, his Socialist books lost much of their bite, yet his vision of a healthy, coöperative society, of politics not of power but of principle, continues to inspire socially concerned undergraduates. Nor are the dons left untouched by his example, for he succeeded in being a scholar who practiced his learning, whose domain was not limited to the tutorial professorial chair but stretched on to include the republic of laborers and politicians.

I had met Tawney only once, over after-dinner coffee at Oxford. As a person, he reminded one of Socrates at his most ironical. (His humility was overpowering and exasperating; when an undergraduate asked him a question about enclosures, a subject on which he was an authority, he said, "No, no, I'm sure you know the field better than I do.") And, like Socrates, he would either be absolutely silent or deliver an endless monologue. Indeed, he gave the impression of being a Platonic Idea of the absent-minded scholar; he would put his glasses on his forehead and then be unable to find them, his brown tweed suit always looked as if it had been slept in, and his untidiness was so thoroughgoing that one expected matches to explode when he reached for them to light his pipe. But whether or not he had fire in his pockets, there was nothing about him to suggest the revolutionary which he actually was.

Tawney, the recent graduate of Oxford setting out on his revolutionary, almost evangelical mission of education, is glimpsed in a commemorative portrait that H. P. Smith, the tutorial secretary for the Delegacy for Extra-Mural Studies, Oxford, wrote for the Delegacy's journal. It tells how Tawney threw himself into the development of the Oxford Tutorial Classes Committee, an extra-mural body for adult education, whose work — which still continues —has influenced the course that English society has taken. He brought the fruits of learning to people at large first by talking and teaching at working-men's clubs in East London, and in the textile country of the north, where he also organized classes for the Lancashire workers. One of his old students, looking back, remembered a number of scenes:

First [Smith quoted], in the classroom at the Sutherland Institute: a heated discussion on surplus value is taking place. A pertinacious Marxian, arguing with the tutor, challenges point after point of his exposition, until at length, baffled but not defeated, the student retires from the tussle, saying to the tutor: "It's no use; when I point my gun at you, you hop from twig to twig like a little bird" — and laughter comes to ease the strain. A more sociable scene in the same room: the class meeting is over, and we sit at ease, taking tea and biscuits provided by members' wives. Talk ranges free and wide — problems of philosophy, evolution, politics, literature. Then R. H. T. reads to us Walt Whitman's "When Lilacs Last in the Dooryard Bloom'd;" this moves a student to give us his favourite passage from the same source: "Pioneers! O Pioneers!" Another follows, quoting from a poem of Matthew Arnold that evidently has bitten him, one ending with the magic line, "the unplumb'd, salt, estranging sea." And for some of us as we sit listening, a new door opens.

Tawney's students soon became the center of a lively educational movement. They started giving talks and classes of their own, modelled on their master's. Under Tawney's direction, the North Staffordshire Miners' Higher Education Movement was launched, and the miners were now enrolled in the movement of voluntary learning and teaching. The scheme, a crusade, culminated a few decades later in the foundation of the University of Keele, in Staffordshire, which is still only one of eighteen institutions of higher learning in all England. Tawney's genius for teaching (copies of his pupils' essays bearing his corrections still serve as examples to young tutors), his relationship with his students (while impatient of sham, he was pastoral in his treatment of his classes), his ability to impart something more than knowledge ("He made manifest a new power in those he taught: the power to shape their own educational activities as adult men and women with their own interests and responsibilities"), his involvement in the social ideals that the classes represented, all helped to make his work a success, to extend the narrow horizons of English aristocratic learning, and to hold out a promise of mass education for a day when there might be greater and greater participation of the people in the government.

The Tawney of the early days [Smith concluded] has become a legend among working-class students in this country. He joined the ranks at the outbreak of hostilities in 1914 and stayed there: it was his way of practicing the equality that he talked. . . . Severely wounded on the Somme, Tawney was brought to hospital in Oxford. There at the Examination Schools he used to lie with piles of books around him, and hot ash dropping from his pipe to his bed. The nurses were scared at his burnt sheets. Another well-authenticated story, this time of the W.E.A. Summer School, is that one of his students . . . decided to honour the occasion of an Oxford college opening its doors to the working classes by coming to Balliol in top-hat and frock-coat. After all, it was his Sunday best, and as an S.D.F.-er [a member of the Social Democratic Federation] he knew that . . . such a garb was indispensable to his preaching of Marx. And so the midnight club was in full swing, the argument was fascinating all participants, the air was thick with smoke, and nobody noticed, until it was too late, that Tawney was emptying his pipe into the silk top-hat on the table beside him. . . .

He set out his thoughts [in an article] on the work in which he was engaged. It is the clearest statement I know of what he stood for in his early days as a tutorial class tutor: "One may suggest that when the wheels have ceased rumbling and the dust has settled down, when the first generation of historians has exhausted the memoirs and the second has refuted the memoirs by the documents, and the time has come for the remorseless eye of imagination to be turned on the first two turbulent decades of the twentieth century, it is perhaps less in the world of political and economic effort than in the revival among large masses of men of an Idea that their dominant *motif* will be found. . . . The minds of an ever-growing number of men and women are passing through one of these mysterious bursts of activity which make some years as decisive as generations, and of which measurable changes in the world of fact are the consequence rather than the cause. May that wonderful spring not be premature! It is as though a man labouring with a pick in a dark tunnel had caught a gleam of light and had redoubled his efforts to break down the last screen. The attack on the mere misery of poverty is falling into its place as one part of a determination that there shall be a radical reconstruction of human relationships. . . . It is surely a very barren kind of pedantry which would treat education as though it were a closed compartment within which principles are developed and experiments tried undisturbed by the changing social currents of the world around. The truth is that educational problems cannot be considered in isolation from the aspirations of the great bodies of men and women for whose sake alone it is that educational problems are worth considering at all. . . . The majority of men — one may hope an increasing majority — must live by working. Their work must be of different kinds, and to do different kinds of work they need specialized kinds of professional preparation. Doctors, lawyers, engineers, plumbers, and masons must, in fact, have trade schools of different kinds. . . . If persons whose work is different require, as they do, different kinds of professional instruction, that is no reason why one should be excluded from the common heritage of civilization of which the other is made free by a university education, and from which, *ceteris paribus*, both, irrespective of their occupations, are equally capable, as human beings, of deriving spiritual sustenance. Those who have seen the inside both of lawyers' chambers and of coal mines will not suppose that of the inhabitants of these places of gloom the former are more constantly inspired by the humanities than are the latter. . . ."

If Tawney the historian, by questions and hypotheses, made old facts give new answers, Namier (a little like Austin) invented a new method to abolish debate and get all the answers once and for all. For the first, the "why" was only a searchlight, for the second a floodlight. Time and again during my encounters with historians, I had come across remarks such as "Namier, perhaps, has found the *ultimate* way of doing history," "Namier believed that just as you can't send up a satellite into space without twentieth-century mathematics, so you can't write history with outmoded nineteenth-century psychology; as soon as this truth is grasped, all the histories written thus far will become dated," and "If Namier had his way, history would become a perfect science and a perfect art. All controversies would cease, and we would know as much historical truth as is humanly possible, without being constantly worn down with doubt and uncertainty." In the minds of the professional academics, he seemed to occupy the position of God, and if they criticized him, it was often more in the spirit of theologians than in the spirit of atheists. Everywhere one turned, whether to literary, diplomatic, philosophical, or psychological historians, whether to Marxist or Conservative, Namier's name was magic. It was alarming and unsettling. To Carr, Namier was "the greatest British historian to emerge on the academic scene since the First World War;" to Berlin, "an historian who psychoanalyzed the past;" to Miss Wedgwood, "perhaps the best historical writer in our time." Toynbee, who had told me that he had almost nothing in common with Namier, had nevertheless said of him, "I worshipped him. He was a big man with a big mind."

Namier has been called a Marx of history, a Freud of history, a Darwin of history. These, like all epithets, are false, and yet contain a grain of truth. Namier attributed the causes of men's actions, like Marx, to something besides their professed motives; like Freud, to subterranean springs; and, like Darwin, to something beyond the mind and its ideas. His spiritual fathers were very imposing, yet when Namier was not writing European or diplomatic history he concentrated his great gifts and genius on studying — or recruiting other great historians to study with him — a period of English Parliament, in exhaustive detail; the last ten years of his life were spent in doing research and writing, with the help of a staff of four, three volumes in the series the "History of Parliament," a sort of *Who's Who* of Members of Parliament who sat in the House of Commons from the Middle Ages to the present century. Namier's own *Who's Who* was to contain a study of nineteen hundred and sixty-four Members in the Parliaments between 1754 and 1790.

Namier's pupil, Taylor, in composing a touching and evaluative epitaph for the *Observer,* succeeded in both justifying and criticizing Namier's narrow preoccupations. He tipped his hat to the master's "unique place" in the world of history, and acknowledged that whatever subject Namier touched his genius transfigured. The nineteenth-century Whig historians had seen democratic Britain as emerging out of the conflict between liberty and despotism. According to them, during the reigns of George I and II liberty had made such inroads on despotism that early Hanoverian politics were polarized between Whigs and Tories, the two kings serving as idle, if handsome, figureheads. George III, however, at the prompting of one of his malign ministers, Lord Bute, was supposed to have reverted to the personal monarchy, costing England the American colonies. Taylor noted that Namier went behind this orthodoxy. He examined the contemporary correspondence, he exposed the assumptions on which the backbenchers and their leaders acted, and he succeeded in showing that these men were not working for the victory of any principle, or party in the modern sense of the word, but were seeking promotion and influence — ambitions to be achieved, as at any time before, by serving the king, still the source of power in public affairs. Even more important than this new interpretation was Namier's method for arriving at it, a method since become famous as "Namierization." Instead of forcing the ideals and opinions of the present onto other times, Namier, by relentlessly substituting accurate details for those vague generalizations that interlined the pages of earlier histories, tried to conduct a gigantic opinion poll of his period. Namierization had since been applied by other scholars to other periods from the fifteenth century to the twentieth century. In Taylor's own words:

Where writers had once dealt vaguely with changes in public opinion or national sentiment, Namier went to the grass-roots of politics. He asked such questions as: What determined the conduct of the individual Member of Parliament? How was representation settled, or changed, in the individual constituencies? Why did men go into politics? What did they get out of it? . . .

Namier did not confine himself to the eighteenth century. . . . [He] knew in his blood the complexities of European nationalism and class-conflict; and he interpreted these complexities to English audiences with dazzling clarity. . . .

But Taylor qualified his praise:

Though his collected works make up a formal array on the shelves, none of them is the finished masterpiece which he hoped to write. . . . It was a strange thing about this great man that, while he could use both the microscope and the telescope to equal effect, he never managed the middle range of common day. He was tremendous when he dissected each detail of some seemingly trivial transaction; and just as powerful when he brought the whole sweep of a century or a continent into a single lecture. But he could not provide sustained narrative. His work lacked movement, which many find the stuff of history. It was ponderous and immobile, like the man himself. . . .

All his books are really related essays on a theme; and they all tend to peter out after the first great impulse. . . . With Namier, it was always all or nothing. Either he was trying to absorb every detail of his subject; or he would throw it away. An excess of patience at one moment; and of impatience afterwards.

I was his colleague at Manchester for eight years; and for twenty-six years his close friend. I loved and admired him as a man as well as an historian. We had our differences. I thought that he had an excessive contempt for ideas and principles in history; a contempt all the stranger when one considers how much he sacrificed in his own life from devotion to the idea of Zionism.

He was an inspired lecturer; and a master of English prose-style. He loved England, particularly the traditional England of the governing classes. Most of all he loved the University of Oxford.

I decided to look up Namier's star pupil, John Brooke — said to be the best source of information on Namier's work and the aims of his history — who had inherited the *Who's Who* duties of his teacher. I made an appointment to see him one afternoon in London at the annex of the Institute of Historical Research library, a rather Victorian house where Brooke and the "History of Parliament" had their offices. I arrived a little early, and chatted for a while with a young lady of the Institute. She told me that in 1951 the British Treasury, at Namier's urging, had provided a grant of seventeen thousand pounds a year for twenty years in order to make possible the writing of the "History of Parliament," which had been apportioned among many historians, some of the country's most distinguished scholars being engaged for the work; originally it was hoped that the whole project would be completed within the twenty years. The work had proceeded at a turtle's pace, however. Namier's period alone had taken the great historian and his staff twice as long as had been planned; often it took many weeks to track down the bare essentials — an M.P.'s parents, the place of his birth, his education, and the date and place and circumstances of his death. Presently, the young lady showed me to a small room at the top of a flight of stairs, and said as she left me, "Mr. Brooke is a very eccentric man. When it gets cold, he wears an electric waistcoat plugged into the light socket, and reads aloud to himself."

The room was brimming with books and papers. Peering over a deskful of big boxes of papers and index cards was a short, slight man with a white, pinched face, who was holding in the corner of his mouth, rather nervously, an unlit cigarette in a cigarette holder. He was youthfully dressed in sweater and slacks, but it was impossible to guess at his age. He was Brooke. Drawing up a chair next to Brooke, I asked him to tell me a little bit about Namier's ideas.

"Sir Lewis had no use for theories of history, you know," Brooke said, switching his unlit cigarette to the other corner of his mouth. "He has written only one essay,

'History,' on the subject; it's collected in 'Avenues of History.' He said once that a great historian is he after whom no one can write history without taking him into account. A historian, to be counted great, must change the whole way of scholarship. Because Sir Lewis basically doesn't believe that a historian can ever know the truth—in our time, you know, this sort of humility is nonexistent—his influence at the moment is limited. But fifty years from now *all* history will be done as Sir Lewis does it." Brooke had a high-pitched voice, and as he talked on I became aware that in speaking of Namier he rather eerily switched from the past tense to the present, as though Namier were still alive. "Sir Lewis doesn't believe, you know, that, like sunshine and rain, ideas exist independently of men," Brooke said. "Rather, he believes that behind every idea there is a man, and *he* is history, the idea a mere rationalization; a revolutionary, you know, may think that he is a revolutionary by conviction, but if, as a historian, you delve into his background—his place of birth, his childhood, the sort of people he was reared with—you may find out that he was really rebelling against his father when he later thought he was rebelling against society. Like Marx, Sir Lewis believes that the way men earn their living, provide themselves with food and shelter, has a lot to do with the way they think and act. He does, however, think that the historian should try to get as close to the truth as possible, though if he thinks he knows the truth about the past, he is either humbugging himself or humbugging someone else. For the men, the real stuff of

history, are elusive, as we never have enough material
on them, and even when we do, as in the eighteenth
and nineteenth centuries, we never have the all-important
psychological material."

Brooke paused and shifted his cigarette holder again.
The more he said, the more the small room became filled
with the absent presence. As he talked on into the afternoon, I realized that facing me was not only a historian
but a hagiographer. "The fact that Sir Lewis was an
Eastern European made him an unprejudiced English
observer, you know; he didn't have any English axe to
grind," Brooke said. (Namier was a Polish Jew, born
Bernstein-Namierowski, in Galicia, who did not come to
England until he was nineteen years old.) "You see, most
people approach history with prejudices. Well, Sir Lewis
thought that if you confined yourself to looking at the
lives of people, writing their *biographies,* you were able
somehow — at least you had the chance — to write history with as little prejudice as possible. You know, he
wanted to get away from prejudices and find out what
people were like, what they did, what their motives were.
A historian's job was constantly to ask what vested interest a man might have had in not reporting an incident
accurately, what opportunity he had for reporting it at
all. If a historian failed to scrutinize *all* the motives of
all the people *all* the time, he might brilliantly reconstruct
a typical day of George III and still get every fact wrong.
Characteristically, Sir Lewis's interest was never in the
big men but always in the little men behind the scenes;
he would give me the biographies of big politicians to

do, and take for himself the backbenchers, not in the public eye and with little material. He was for writing the biographies of these men because with biographies there was less chance of a historian's projecting his own ideas into the past and justifying them with facts. For example, in writing about the constitutional struggle in seventeenth-century England, a Communist would see it one way, a Tory in an entirely different way, but if you were simply writing biographies . . ."

He shifted his unlit cigarette once more and went on, "Sir Lewis thinks that the reason for the flood of prejudiced histories is that most historians to this day use nineteenth-century psychology, as though Freud had never lived. Because in history there are no criteria of true and false, as in the natural sciences, no one can really disprove or dismiss these histories that keep on being written and read and accepted." According to Brooke, Namier believed that psychology was as important to history as mathematics was to astronomy, and that without the psychological plane history was two-dimensional; all the historians of the past had spent their time sketching flat characters. Take the great Charles K. Webster, Brooke said, who composed his celebrated works within our lifetime. His histories made no connection between, say, Castlereagh's foreign policy and his insanity, which ended in his suicide, and none between King George III's policy and *his* insanity — between the men as they were and the ideas they had. For Namier, if history had any value, it lay in trying to reconstruct the lives of men from practically nonexistent material. He wished — as far as the evidence allowed — to write history as current events, to view it through the eyes of the characters as they were acting history. Namier wanted to put himself in the shoes of vanished Kennedys and Khrushchevs, and, ignoring all the later happenings, to see them as they were in the process of making decisions.

I asked Brooke why a historian couldn't write both about men and about ideas.

"It is not that Sir Lewis was not interested in the history of ideas," Brooke replied. "He was the last person to deny that, say, Communism influences the way people think, and that we should write about it. But he just thought that anybody could sit down and turn out a history of ideas, anybody could produce a study of Marx and Lenin simply by reading them. It needed far more imagination to get to the psychological springs of these ideas. In this sense, he did discount plans, ideas, and dreams in favor of realities and pressures. In this connection"— here Brooke walked over to a bookshelf that held the complete works of Namier — "there are a couple of very famous paragraphs, you know." And then he read out in his thin voice a passage from Namier's "England in the Age of the American Revolution":

"Why was not representation in the British Parliament — a British Union — offered to the Colonies? Or why, alternatively, was not an American Union attempted, such as had been proposed at the Albany Congress in 1754? This might have freed Great Britain from burdens, responsibilities, and entanglements, and paved the way to Dominion status. Both ideas were discussed at great length and with copious repetition, but mechanical devices, though easily conceived on paper, are difficult to carry into practice when things do not, as it were, of their own accord, move in that direction. There is 'the immense distance between planning and executing' and 'all the difficulty is with the last.' . . . In the end statesmen hardly ever act except under pressure of 'circumstances,' which means of mass movements and of the mental climate in their own circles. But about 1770, the masses in Great Britain were not concerned with America, and the mental and moral reactions of the political circles were running on lines which, when followed through, were bound to lead to disaster.

"The basic elements of the Imperial Problem during the American Revolution must be sought not so much in conscious opinions and professed views bearing directly on it, as in the very structure and life of the Empire; and in doing that the words of Danton should be remembered — *on ne fait pas le procès aux révolutions.* Those who are out to apportion guilt in history have to keep to views and opinions, judge the collisions of planets by the rules of road traffic, make history into something like a column of motoring accidents, and discuss it in the atmosphere of a police court. But whatever theories of 'free will' theologians and philosophers may develop with regard to the individual, there is no free will in the thinking and actions of the masses, any more than in the revolutions of planets, in the migrations of birds, and in the plunging of hordes of lemmings into the sea."

Brooke tenderly returned the book to the shelf and resumed his seat behind the cluttered desk. "You know," he said, "there has been a bitter debate going on between Taylor and Trevor-Roper about Taylor's latest book, 'The Origins of the Second World War.' Everyone has been wishing that Sir Lewis were alive to settle it. I have no doubt about his sentence. The main issues between them are: Did Hitler have a plan? Did the masses have free will not to follow him? Trevor-Roper invokes Sir Lewis's name when, in his review of Taylor's 'Origins,' he says 'what devastating justice it would have received' at Sir Lewis's hands. I think if Sir Lewis were alive he might object to Taylor's provocative style, the lacunae in his arguments, but nevertheless, as the paragraphs I read to you suggest, he would come out firmly on the side of Taylor, for his thesis. When Alan Bullock's brilliant biography of Hitler was published, Sir Lewis and I had a long conversation about it. I said to him that for me Bullock didn't answer two essential questions: Why, if Hitler was so mentally unstable, was he able to get such a hold on the German people, and why — this is an allied question — did the German people follow him as they did? Sir Lewis said that he agreed with my criticism, and that, unlike Bullock, he didn't think that the answers to these questions could be found in the character of Hitler. They were to be found in the German people as a whole — in the *pressure of circumstances.* He himself, in his 'Diplomatic Prelude,' had tried to do precisely this — shift the emphasis from Hitler to the German nation. In any case, Sir Lewis thought extremely highly of Taylor's scholarship, and such criticisms as

'Taylor didn't give much weight to the death of the six million Jews' wouldn't have caused Sir Lewis to turn a hair; after all, their death had little to do with the origins of the war. Indeed, if Sir Lewis were now living, his presence would be enough to prevent Trevor-Roper from laying into Taylor. His very existence deterred people from writing bad reviews and bad books. But" — Brooke sighed — "his first love was not diplomatic but parliamentary history."

"Why was it that the Freud of history took up the stick-in-the-mud subject of Parliament?" I asked.

"Sir Lewis, you know, was essentially an existential historian," Brooke replied. "Here, he believed, were the people, here their relationships; they together made up the circumstances of history. If history was *not* to be a catalogue of suppositions — it became that in the hands of most historians — it had to be *solidly* based on minute facts. A historian had to address himself to facts about people who *mattered* — and in his eighteenth century the people who *really* mattered were the politicians. For in Parliament and Parliament alone had people made politically important decisions. The workers, the peasants, collectively, had hardly ever mattered, except in times of rebellion. But since all rebellions were short-lived, a historian rarely had to take notice of them. His method, I agree, was perhaps better suited to nineteenth-century Europe — the material for it was more abundant — but he settled on the eighteenth-century English Parliament because at heart he was an imperialist, and he wanted to know how the American empire had been broken up."

"An imperialist!" I exclaimed.

"Imperialist, yes. Imperialist," Brooke said. "But the reasons for his imperialism are too complicated for me to go into."

I said I had plenty of time.

"Don't you know anything about Sir Lewis as a man?" he asked.

I said, "Not much." I knew a little bit about Namier through a conversation I had had with Toynbee, who had been at Balliol with him. "Lewis was the freshest thing that happened to Balliol in my time," Toynbee had said. "We got on very well, perhaps because we were both interested in queer, faraway places — he in his home, Eastern Europe, I in the Orient. Perhaps his alien background partly explains the totally original outlook he had on things all his life. Even as an undergraduate, he succeeded in illuminating the world with flashes of insight. Once, he came up to me in the college quadrangle and told me that in Poland there was little relation between the Bible and the development of her language. This simple fact made me realize instantly how different life in Poland must be from life in England, for here the Bible was the fountainhead of the literature, a great armory of our language. Perhaps I should have known such simple facts, but I didn't. After Oxford, we became more and more opposite; he started applying to history the same microscopic method that the rabbis had applied to the study of the Scriptures, while I addressed myself to larger and larger questions. Yet he told me once, 'Toynbee, I study the individual leaves, you the tree. The rest of the historians study the clusters of branches, and we both think *they* are wrong.' For a while, I sent him my chapters, like those on Palestine — he was a great Zionist — and he never failed to mark them up with notes so copious that it was barely possible to read the manuscript. One day, when the differences in our historical treatment became too great, he returned one of my Palestine chapters without a single comment. But years later, when I met him in lower Regent Street, the first thing he said to me was, 'Toynbee, about that footnote in the Palestine chapter . . .'"

"Let me begin from the beginning," Brooke said now. "Of course his wife, Lady Namier, knows him best as a person" — Brooke was back in the present tense — "but next to her I suppose I am closest to him. Most people find Sir Lewis impossible to get to know. For one thing, he doesn't talk to anyone about his deep convictions, lest they be misunderstood, and, for another, not being a very social person, he doesn't have much opportunity for talking. He has no patience with small talk, so if he doesn't know people, he is silent, and if he knows them, he talks endlessly, but never ranges far from his subject, which is why he has a reputation for being a crashing bore. In fact, Sir Lewis talked himself out of a chair at Oxford. The dons were afraid that he would not be good company in the common room. This belief was so universal that it even got into the obituaries. Also, the manner of his speech was a deterrent. He couldn't really pronounce the 'th' — but then some Englishmen can't either — but the thing that made his speech most difficult was the shortening of the 'a's; he said 'feather' instead of 'father.' And many people were put off by his grim expression, which seldom broke into a smile — but when it did, it was wonderful. Yet, you know, Sir Lewis is a very engaging man. In winter, he comes into the office in a soft hat, but if it's raining he may wear a felt cap. He usually comes in at ten o'clock in the morning and leaves at six. He also does a lot of work at home. He works very hard. He never reads very much outside his subject. It is difficult to imagine him having an evening with a detective story or a novel. In fact, he is not a very broad man. He never listens to music or goes to the theatre. He hates the dilettante, and perhaps that's another reason he is considered a bit of a bore. When he was alive, we used to work in the basement of the Historical Institute — they wanted to move us to the annex then, but they didn't dare while he was alive. I used to sit with another assistant and a secretary in a large room, and he occupied the next room, which he always kept very bare; there were just the usual books all around, and these boxes, and this armchair you're sitting in — that was all. The way we worked was to go through all the manuscripts and printed sources looking for names of Members of Parliament, and first we would do a factual survey on where the M.P. lived and when he died — that was all put on one set of cards. Then, on the second set, we put where we got all the material, and then, with the help of these sets of cards, we wrote up the biographies. I wrote mine very quickly. He stewed and labored for days and days. He was so neurotic about his manuscripts that he was always fearful that they would go up in smoke. Even though I sat in the next room, he asked me to stop smoking. When I asked him why, he said, 'I'm afraid of fire.' You know, Sir Lewis is a strange man. But he is not at all moody. Not being able to sleep is his greatest curse. He used to come to me in the morning and say, 'I didn't sleep very much last night. I can't write a word today.' He might have as many as four such days in a week. Of course, it didn't affect the quality of his research, but it did slow him down. I can't sleep at night, either. I'm physically tired, but my mind is very active."

I asked Brooke if he and Namier had a lot of other things in common.

"Of course, I am of his historical persuasion," he said, "but a whole generation divides him and his politics from me and mine. He was seventy-two when he died, and I am forty-one. While he grew up to be a natural conservative in imperial Eastern Europe, I grew up in a Left Wing, Left Book Club, Spanish Civil War atmosphere, and ended up being a Socialist. I first met Sir Lewis when he was a professor at Manchester and I chose to do his special topic. We met for two hours at a time twice a week. After that, he adopted me as his star pupil and brought me with him to London when he came to do the 'History of Parliament,' and after that I saw him every day. How he hated change! When I started attending his class at Manchester, I happened to arrive before anyone else, and took the first chair on his left in the semicircle. My second time, I came late, but he insisted that I sit in the same chair, saying 'I don't like change.' Here in London, he always lunched at the same restaurant — Bertorelli's — at the same table, at the same hour, and almost always alone. Tea we always had together. His routine was by no means the full extent of his conservatism. He would have nothing to do with television. He would never watch it, he refused to have it in his house, and he refused to appear on it. I'm sure twenty-five years ago he was against the motorcar. His personal conservatism perhaps explains his conservative politics. But, you will ask, what about his *imperialism?* Well, I think he was just anti-liberal, you know. He didn't have a high opinion of the achievements of the human race, and he thought the British Empire was humane. Unlike the liberals, he didn't believe in any sort of progress; he didn't think things were getting better and better. It wasn't that he didn't want to reform decrepit institutions — he just hated to see them go. For example, he didn't want the House of Lords abolished, even though he knew it was not what it had been in the past. He felt we ought to leave it to the life force to slowly adapt the institutions to the times. He felt the same way about religion. He never talked about that to anyone — except me, when I got to know him very well. Then he told me that he believed in an interdenominational God. The strange thing was that, conservative or no, next to Freud he was most influenced by Marx."

I stretched a little and stood up, but I could tell by Brooke's tone that I had stood up a little too early; he had more to say. So I sat down again.

"As I look back on Sir Lewis's life," he was saying, "the thing that is perhaps strangest of all is his two-sided output, which almost suggests Siamese twins at work. First, there are these short — embarrassingly short — historical essays; they contain only Sir Lewis's brief conclusions, rather like the answers at the back of the arithmetic book. And you know that these are answers not to small historical sums but to long — very long — ones, sometimes covering a hundred-year stretch of history. Second, there are these other histories, big histories, on which Sir Lewis's reputation rests, and they are so dense and detailed — day-by-day historical sums — that one is hard put to it to find any conclusions. And *these* great books are really memorable for — among other things, of course — not ever having been completed. These unfinished histories put one in mind of Michelangelo's 'imprisoned' statues, in which the thought strains to be free of the stone. Sir Lewis began chiselling at these big books in the twenties, by going to America to look at Colonial history, to find out how the empire had broken up. But one American historian, Charles McLean Andrews, sent him back to England, telling him that the best contribution he could make would be to study what happened to the empire from the English side. Here in England, he stumbled on huge archives of two famous eighteenth-century politicians — nine hundred and twenty-eight volumes of Hardwicke papers, and five hundred and twenty-three volumes of Newcastle papers. Romney Sedgwick, who later became his closest friend, had partly looked through the collections, but, being a civil servant, had found no time to do anything with them. Indeed, no one had thoroughly, exhaustively examined them from the point of view of parliamentary history. Sir Lewis started digging through this material in the Manuscript Room of the British Museum, and began writing his masterly 'The Structure of Politics at the Accession of George III.' It was published in 1929. The 'Structure' was mainly an analytical work, and he was going to follow it up with a narrative history of 'England in the Age of the American Revolution,' covering the years from 1760 to 1783, but he published only one volume of the narrative, which was so detailed that it stopped at 1762. Now, if he had completed this project — given a volume to every two years — it would have taken a dozen more volumes, but he never got around to them. In the thirties, when he might have done some more work on the Revolution, he became obsessed with Zionism and gave most of his time to that. After the war, he started to write again, and from the wave of contemporary memoirs and diaries he produced his 'Diplomatic Prelude, 1938-39.' Well, you know how things were right after the war. Even before the study was reviewed, there rushed out from the Foreign Offices and the politicians' pens a flood of more memoirs and more diplomatic notes. Then he started rewriting this book altogether; he never finished it, either. After that, he took up another great work, a biography of one Charles Townshend — you know, the grandson of the so-called Turnip Townshend, of the eighteenth century — in which, for the first time, he was going to use explicitly his Freudian principles. That, too, was never finished, and his great dream, which took shape about the same time, of writing an individual biography of nineteen hundred and sixty-four Members of Parliament in the Namier period, and exploring the network of connections between them — well, death cut it short." Brooke abruptly stopped.

"Why didn't he finish things?" I asked.

"Well," he said, "it's a mystery."

"Do you have any theories about it?" I said.

"There are many things I can say about it," he continued. "First — a metaphor. Think of a historian as a walker on the road of history. Most historians walk straight along the road; they begin at one end and come out at the other, without looking left or right. Well, Sir Lewis never walked a step without looking in every direction; in fact, he spent all his life in byways. Once, we went to Bowood, Lord Lansdowne's country house in Wiltshire. There were boxes of documents, and we had only a day. We divided the boxes up and started going through the documents. I got through mine three times as fast as Sir Lewis got through his; I would look at a heading and more or less decide from that whether there was anything in it of importance to the history of Parliament — whether it was just a private letter or an official paper — but not so Sir Lewis. He would read about half the document carefully before making up his mind. Perhaps I missed something — I don't think I missed very much — but he missed *nothing*. Many of the details he thus dug up turned out to be irrelevant, but unless he had explored all the byways, he might never have written his *definitive* works, for before he wrote his big books he took into account *every* discoverable fact; no one could ever supersede him by turning up new ones. The other way he insured the production of a definitive work was by sheer craftsmanship. The pains he took and his incredible judgment about words made him the best writer of history since Gibbon and Macaulay. But being a foreigner and also an impeccable stylist slowed him down — it would have slowed down the gods. Also, in his later years his right arm became paralyzed, which meant that in the museums and libraries he couldn't copy down the material he needed. He had to resort to a very cumbersome method of copying down only titles and page numbers, and the texts later had to be transcribed by his secretary. What's more, he could compose only at the typewriter, and since he didn't know the touch system, he would hammer out his first draft with one or two fingers. He used shorthand such as 'P-l-m-n-t' for 'Parliament,' 'k' for 'king,' and 't' for 'the.' The draft had to be recopied by his secretary before he could even revise. And *this* process had to be repeated about a dozen times, since ten or twelve drafts were not unusual for Sir Lewis. Take the different ways that Sir Lewis, the master, and I, a sort of average historian, had of writing. We both had boxes of index cards and innumerable folders of typed extracts from documents. Suppose Sir Lewis and I were writing on Grenville and Burke, respectively — both big men in our period. I would go carefully through my boxes, sort out the material, make up my mind about what was important, and, once I sat down at the typewriter, type it out very quickly. Sir Lewis, on the other hand, would sit at his typewriter without knowing what he was going to do with the material. He would go back and forth between his boxes and folders and his typewriter. It would be a constant process of writing and rewriting, shaping and reshaping, agony and more agony — and the biography was not more than a seven-thousand-word job. Nobody could be more sensitive than he as a scale on which words could be weighed, but I think that now and again he was pedantic about style. For example, you could never shake him in his belief that the noun ought to come before the pronoun: 'George I, when he was king . . .' Once I pointed out to him a *Times* first leader that read, 'In his speech, Chou En-lai said . . .' to make the point that sometimes in good writing the noun did come after the pronoun. His comment was simply 'The *Times* is deteriorating.' This business about nouns and pronouns also slowed his reading. 'I am a slow reader because — ' he would say to me, and then read out some such phrase as 'In his view . . .' 'How do I know,' he would shout, 'who it is that "his" refers to?' I think he really was a slow reader. As if poring over details, writing slowly, and reading slowly were not enough, Sir Lewis went to enormous trouble over evidence; he never took anything for granted. For example, it was accepted by historians that the papers of Lord Bute, a Prime Minister of George III, were burned in a fire on his estate in Luton, Bedfordshire; this belief had been handed down through a long tree of history books. Even a historical commission, which had gone to the horse's mouth, a descendant of Bute's, had got this answer. But Sir Lewis was not put off. He sought out the descendant, and before the chap knew it both he and Sir Lewis were at the family solicitor's office, rummaging through papers. Of course, they found the Bute papers."

Outside, London had become dark; we had been talking for a long while. I stood up. Brooke came downstairs with me. On the way, I asked him to tell me a bit about himself.

"I've just completed and sent to press all the biographies of M.P.s in Sir Lewis's period," he said. "Now I'm writing a general survey of conclusions, which I hope to finish within the next three or four months. I'm a hard worker. Ordinarily, I work from early in the morning until late at night. I start work at seven in the morning, work until breakfast, at eight, and get to the office at a quarter to ten. I have a sandwich lunch brought to me at my desk, go home about five-thirty, and then do two or three hours after dinner. I have a lot of books at home. You see, Sir Lewis left me all his books, and I have taken many of them home, because this office wasn't built for a library and they were afraid the floor would collapse." We were at the door now. "I'm married. I have three children — a son of ten and twins of seven, a boy and a girl."

I asked Brooke a final question, which I had been turning in my mind, but which I had kept waiting, fearing that it might be indelicate to ask of a hagiographer. By this time, however, I had become convinced that no question could disturb Brooke's picture of Namier. "Did he apply to himself the same methods of analysis that he applied to all the nineteen hundred and sixty-four M.P.s and to Charles Townshend?" I asked.

Brooke took the question as I had expected — calmly. "Yes, he did. In fact, he spent many years in psychoanalysis, but Lady Namier would like to tell you all that herself. She is writing a biography of him, and although ordinarily wives are not the best biographers, she is an exception. She is a most extraordinary woman, and well fitted in every way to be the wife of Sir Lewis."

Namier, I discovered, was still listed in the London Directory, and I rang Lady Namier at his number. Since she was just then going abroad for a short rest, I arranged to meet her on her return and, in the meantime, looked to Namier's critics. As it happened, Namier's demise did not serve as a deterrent to criticism. Indeed, even in his lifetime many voices had been raised, though always respectfully, against his fragmentary, hairsplitting method, and against his tendency and that of his "disciples" to denigrate, if not to discount, the force of ideas behind men's actions. His critics had argued that while his method was admirably suited to eighteenth-century England, where ideas were at a low temperature, it was ill-suited to, for instance, the Puritan Revolution, whose ideological heat couldn't be explained away in terms of petty self-interest. Herbert Butterfield, Master of Peterhouse, Cambridge, a mostly analytic dry-biscuit historian, thought he had succeeded in sifting the wheat from the chaff in Namier's thought. Namierites might — indeed, did — object to Butterfield the winnower, claiming that he had a second role, that of a Christian thinker, which disqualified him as a balanced critic. (What was the sacred stuff of Christianity, its propelling force, they asked. Not mundane facts, not every individual motive, but large ideals — the concepts of God and the hereafter, the institution of the Church, the bond of Communion.) But he was not so easily dismissed. He paid his respects to the artistry, the ceaseless slavery that carried the results of Namier's definitive, if tedious, researches — those sentences that stood like so many gnomic guards around his ambition and his reputation — but still he assailed Namier, at times successfully thumbing his nose at the spit and polish, the swagger, of the bright battle line. Indeed, when Namier was living and terrorizing the historical scene from the Delphic pages of the *Times Literary Supplement*, Butterfield had boldly issued a book, "George III and the Historians," in which he attacked Namier and termed his school "the most powerfully organized squadron in our historical world at the present time." With the throne freshly vacated, Butterfield was no less audacious. He appeared on the B.B.C.'s Third Programme and delivered, more in the style of Brutus than in that of Mark Antony, an estimation of Namier and his work, and while Namierites felt certain that he little understood their Caesar, non-Namierites sent up a cheer for the speaker's perceptiveness and clear thinking. Many of those who listened to him found it hard to resist his boyish, intimate voice, which burned with the ardor of a people's preacher. Always giving chapter and verse, now it praised Namier's style ("Sometimes Namier uses a figure of speech so effectively that it acquires a solemn ring, like a sound in an empty cavern. . . . But when he stands farthest of all from the scene, like a pitying God who watches human beings for a moment in love, he reaches the sort of music that we find in the thrilling parts of the Old Testament: 'For in the life of every man comes a night when at the ford of the stream he has to strive "with God and with men;" and if he prevails and receives the blessing of the father-spirit, he is henceforth free and at peace'"); now it praised Namier's insight into people, events, and situations ("The thing that carried him far above all routine historians, and could not be transmitted to anybody else, was a penetrating kind of insight. It appears in swift impressions of people: as when Metternich is described as 'that rococo figure in porcelain, stylish and nimble, and in appearance hollow and brittle.' It shows itself in drastic comments on events: as when he says that 'The eighteenth-century British claim to superiority over the Colonies was largely the result of thinking in terms of personified countries.' We see it in bold pieces of generalization: 'The Anglo-Saxon mind, like the Jewish, is inclined to legalism'; 'The social history of nations is largely moulded by the forms and development of their armed forces'"); now it praised the constructive imagination that lay behind one great work of Namier's, "The Structure of Politics at the Accession of George III" ("Once again, it was the insight that mattered — insight which . . . produced a new landscape for the politics of the year 1760"); and now it praised his uncanny ability as a historian to rise above the present and reach into the future — the dream of all historians ("Even in the midst of controversy, he could take a distant stand, pausing for a moment, and seeing recent events with the eye of a later historian. He caught a glimpse of what later generations might see, and wrote for a moment once again like a pitying God. There is a moving example of this in an essay entitled 'Memoirs Born of Defeat' . . . in the book 'Europe in Decay': 'There is a great deal to be said in defense of the French statesmen and generals of the inter-war period, but on a plane different from that on which most of them choose to argue the case'"). But then, like spadefuls of earth on the grave, fell the "yets"s. *Yet* the voice, with a thin rumble of thunder, denounced Namier's style ("Some of his large-scale works remind me of broken Gothic — with gargoyles and glimpses of cherubs — the whole involving a mixture of styles which he was too impatient to turn into continuity or assimilate to an architectural design. It seems to me, moreover, that he did not care to give much of himself to the construction of historical narrative"); and *yet* it expressed reservations about the treatment of people, events, and situations ("Namier used a raw method of narration, convenient for technical historians who like to have their materials neat; but I am not sure that even technical historians do not need to be warned about its dangers. What he gives us is chiefly a dense patchwork of quotations from contemporary letters, and so on. But, in the first place, when high spots from such documents are telescoped into a short space, and not accompanied by exposition — not accompanied by a type of narrative that is more than factual — then the craziness of human beings tends to be accentuated by reason of what has been left out. We are liable to lose sight of that nine-tenths of a man which is more normal human nature. I wonder if many people have not come to feel that the world of 1760 was sillier than the world of most other periods — and full of sillier people — because of the danger that lies in this technique so long as the historian is withholding himself from part of his function. . . . To the technical historian I would say that history is not to be produced by drawing direct lines between one document and another, for each must be referred back to a man and a mind from which it came. Particularly in the world of politics it happens to be the case that men say things and write things with what I should call a 'tactical' intent. If you take these as a record of a man's opinions, you are bound to get the contradictions which made Namier feel that here was the craziness of what he called 'historical comedy' "); *yet* it denounced the unconstructive aspects of Namier's work ("I wonder if I am the only person in the country who wishes that, after 1930, he had worked rather on great statesmen not too near the present time, or produced a narrative of higher politics — including governmental policy — in the reign of George III. Indeed, sometimes I wish that all the constituencies and elections and Members of Parliament in George III's reign had been exhaustively treated, so that we could return to political history again — to the study of statesmanship and things that enlarge the mind"); and *yet,* finally, it denounced Namier's historical viewpoint ("He went too far in his brilliant thesis that the actions of men acquire their rationality and purposefulness only in the thinking that is done after the event").

In his funeral oration, Butterfield took away with one hand what he gave with the other, until he left one with the impression that he was indeed an honorable man.

Now and again, by legerdemain, he slipped into the text his own views on how the historian should rule his material. Phrases like "technical historian," "higher politics," "the study of statesmanship and things that enlarge the mind" suggested a way of approaching history that was peculiar to Butterfield. And he was not at all reluctant to use the opportunity to make his code of history more explicit. "I doubt," he declaimed, "whether history can be properly written unless one has a sort of sense for the evidence that is not there. . . . Each document requires one to conduct a special transaction with it, and needs to be interpreted in the light of everything else that can be gathered round it. When eighteenth-century fathers write bitterly about the egotism of their sons, we must not imagine that here we have evidence for the selfishness of the younger men. Once everything is put together, we may need actually to invert the construction of the passage in question. It may turn out to be only additional evidence of the father's own egotism." And "Behind the hesitations and contradictions of men there is generally, at some level, a certain stability of mind and purpose. The standing evidence for this element of stable purpose needs to be weighed against the day-by-day evidence which often shows only the cross-purposes and vacillations."

These intimations of his own theories of history, and my wish to clear up the muddle about Namier, made me decide to look Butterfield up in Cambridge. He invited me to have lunch with him at twelve-thirty on a

Saturday. I arrived in Cambridge half an hour early, and spent the free time going through Peterhouse, which is the oldest college at Cambridge, and which in recent years has had connected with it some brilliant historians — the Reverend Dr. David Knowles, Professor Denis Brogan, Professor of Economic History Michael Postan, Denis Mack Smith, and Butterfield himself, author of sixteen books and a professor and former Vice-Chancellor of the university. After a quick tour, I walked across the street to the Master's lodgings, a rather old-looking house, symmetrical in its design. I was let in by a maid, and shown up a carpeted staircase to an oak-panelled study with a fireplace, a large desk, and many books.

Butterfield, who was born with the century, and who has round shoulders, silvery hair, and overpowering charm, shuffled in, wearing horn-rimmed glasses and an informal dull-gray suit. I shook the Master's hand and sat down with him on a sofa in front of the fireplace. He was gracious and unassuming, and in appearance he suggested a country parson. A Player's cigarette, however, hung from his lower lip, and threatened to fall off at any moment. He certainly didn't look like Brutus, even less like St. John the Baptist, yet as he talked on into the afternoon, his voice once in a while had an uncomfortable ring of crying in the wilderness, and his tone, though never prophetic, was sometimes jarringly out of tune with the temper of the times.

First, after a little prompting from me, he talked about Namier: "I don't suppose anyone has written Namier a more rapturous tribute than I have. He was a giant —

perhaps the only giant in our time. He was a historian's historian, because his research was all-embracing and flawless, his artistry imposing. He took a certain view of the eighteenth century, and I agree with him. But as a *teacher,* and a *master* of the college, I have to deplore his method. If we were to teach history by Namier's method, if we were to train students to do research and try to write history as Namier did, then history as a part of education would cease to exist. Already his influence has been pernicious. In some colleges, people have burrowed themselves like moles into smaller and smaller holes — in a little biographical hole here, in a little diplomatic hole there — and their minds have ceased to develop. As far as I am concerned, the point of teaching history to undergraduates is to turn them into future public servants and statesmen, in which case they had better believe in ideals, and not shrink from having ideas and policies and from carrying their policies through. We mustn't cut the ground from under them by teaching that all ideas are rationalizations. In brief, we must take a *statesmanlike* view of the subject. No doubt Namier would smile at this — I know it sounds priggish — but I happen to think history is a school of wisdom and of statesmanship. If these undergraduates are going to become professional historians, I like *them* best when they feel at ease in many periods of history, when they are in the classical tradition of scholarship, like Sir George — G. N. — Clark, the historian of seventeenth-century Europe. Have you met him?"

I said I had. G. N. Clark was a stalwart of the English scholarly Establishment. He had written an introduction to "The New Cambridge Modern History" and, at a luncheon party, launched the fifteen-volume "Oxford History of England." He had been a professor at both universities. When he was at Cambridge, scholars used to consult "G. N." in the same spirit as the Greeks consulted the oracle. To meet "G. N.," who turned out to be a very cautious, canny Yorkshire gentleman of seventy-two, I had gone all the way to King's Sutton, a typical English village lying near the pastoral Cotswold Hills north of Oxford, where at present he is living and writing a history of medicine. Huddling over a primitive gas stove, G. N. had quietly delivered his classical notions of scholarship. "In my view, history should be written without any thesis to prove. It should be a collective, coöperative effort to search out the evidence and write it up in felicitous language. But nowadays scholars dash off books with incredible mistakes in them, and other scholars wait to catch them out in reviews, when by reading the manuscript in advance of publication they could have corrected them, cleared them up. In times past, when history was not done by everybody but by a small band of devotees, there was no impetus to controversy. But the growth — by leaps and bounds — of the layman's knowledge of history has made of scholars prima donnas; they can't resist playing up to their new-found audience. I myself learned that controversy did not lead anywhere quite early on. When I was an undergradu-

ate, we had a very eminent speaker at a college society —
I don't want to mention his name and get embroiled in
controversy, the very thing I disapprove of. After he had
finished speaking, like a typical undergraduate — and
scholars today — I stood up and made a pretty little attack on his speech, which I concluded by quoting a line
from Gilbert and Sullivan's 'Patience': 'Nonsense, yes,
perhaps — but oh, what precious nonsense!' To my great
amazement, the eminent speaker dissolved into tears.
Since then I have found myself in only two *minor* controversies; one of my opponents, poor chap, died before he
had a chance to reply." G. N.'s noncontroversial, "committee" approach to history had a long and august line
of descent. In a sense, it was the classical way of doing
history. But the rub was that committee history, such
as "The New Cambridge Modern History," tended, as
some critics had pointed out, to be static and dull (it
took on the quality of rows upon rows of evenly clipped
hedges in the land of the gentry), because our discovery
in this century of the subterranean impulses behind men's
thought and action had shattered the simple, the har-
monious, the proportioned, the finished — the classic
— view of the world which that history mirrored, and had
given the interpretive mind an all-important role. Carr,
in "What Is History?," had registered this objection — as
often, in a rather extreme form — when he wrote, "Indeed, if, standing Sir George Clark on his head, I were
to call history 'a hard core of interpretation surrounded
by a pulp of disputable facts,' my statement would, no

doubt, be one-sided and misleading, but no more so, I venture to think, than the original [Clark's] dictum."

Butterfield continued to talk about Namier and Namierites. Puffing every so often at his Player's, which had a permanent place on his lower lip, he casually criticized a couple of Namierites and just a little less casually saluted Taylor. "Namier's titular successor, Brooke, and the Oxford historian Betty Kemp, et cetera, tend to underestimate — although perhaps Namier himself didn't — the part that ideas play in history," Butterfield said. "For example, they say that George III didn't have *any* policies, didn't have *any* ideas. Well, I think even George III had some ideas. But Taylor, Namier's pupil for eight years, is a horse of another color. Do you know, I am one of the few people who even admire his 'Origins of the Second World War'? I have been saying this to all my colleagues. It seems to me that we ought to try to look at technical history as objectively as possible, and I think the contemporary view of history is often the least satisfactory and the most biased. Sometimes the future puts the past into perspective, adds an element to it unknown to the contemporaries. Take the English Reformation. The people who carried out the Reformation and the contemporaries who wrote about it never realized that the enormous price revolution in the sixteenth century — in many cases, prices quadrupled — had been a factor in the Reformation conflicts. It was only later that historians discovered this piece of knowledge. Or simply take the origins of the First World War. The

Englishmen, Frenchmen, and Russians who were living during the war all looked at it purely from their own points of view. It was only later that historians came along and started looking at the origins from all sides, and we found out that the war was not started by the Germans or the Austro-Hungarians but by things like imperial naval rivalry and the Balkan issue — things endemic in the European situation. Similarly, until Taylor, people took the contemporary view — indeed, it is the orthodoxy — that the Second World War was caused by Germany and Hitler. And I think Taylor was right, at least in intention, to come along later and ask himself how the origins of the war looked from English, French, Russian, and German documents. Of course, other people had written from a documentation that was multinational before Taylor, but his book represents a later stage in the development of historiography — namely, the very difficult point where one begins to go over the story without always having in mind the way that the story ended. Also, what Taylor is saying is *not* that Hitler and Germany didn't start the war; he is saying that they didn't start the war *when* the war was started, that Hitler didn't want the war when in fact it came — and that is quite a different thing from saying Hitler didn't want war at all. The book may be full of flaws, but it's more interesting than has been made out. The fact that Taylor fails to condemn Hitler doesn't worry me; it sounds priggish, but I don't think passing judgment is in the province of a technical historian. I think that's God's job, that's God's history — though I don't personally like the term."

And Butterfield went on to define his strange, almost medieval concept of God's history. "In my view, there are two kinds of history: God's history and technical history," he said. "God's history is evaluative; you distribute blame, you judge people, and so on. Technical history is what we all write; you look at the evidence, you draw conclusions. With it you can't really get through to the intimate part of history, to the ninety-nine per cent of history; you can't find out, for example, whether Caesar loved his wife, or whether I am sincere or honest when I say certain things. It sounds priggish, but I think only God can know all that. I am impelled to explain this because these two kinds of history are often confused; St. Augustine's 'City of God' was taken literally in the Middle Ages as technical history, when in fact it was God's history, so this nimble book, in the hands of the zealots, became a literal text."

Butterfield was not the first to divide up the province of history between God and man, one infinite in scope and the other infinitesimal; indeed, the idea of God's history had a long lineage, stretching from the Old Testament, through St. Augustine, to Reinhold Niebuhr and Arnold Toynbee. What was remarkable was that, whatever Butterfield's religious views, they never colored his professional academic history, and, perhaps because he never hitched his lay history to the ecclesiastical wagon, he didn't forfeit his professional colleagues' respect or confidence. But sometime in the middle forties, in the midstream of his historical career (the technical variety), he had felt the need to define and demarcate the two fields, and had done so in his book "Christianity and History." I asked him now why he had suddenly stepped into the murky no man's land of history and religion.

"Sometime during the war, the theologians of Cambridge invited a lay philosopher to lecture on philosophy and Christianity," he replied. "The lectures, coming in the trough of war depression, were such a great success — undergraduates flocked to them — that the theologians decided to follow them up with lectures on history and Christianity. Again they wanted a lay historian, rightly thinking that his pronouncements would carry more weight with the unconverted, but no such historian was forthcoming. I let myself be coaxed into doing it. Since the lectures, I find myself regarded as an authority on the subject, when I am really . . ."

Then Butterfield reluctantly talked a little about his private, religious view of the world. "I am a Nonconformist, a Methodist, but I don't think my belief in Providence, my belief in both original sin and free will — without the one you can't have the other — and the other tenets of my religious faith need come into my writing of technical history, though I often wonder whether Christian views of life don't somewhere make a difference even to the professional historian. I rather think that a Christian would be tied to an idea of personality, which would make a difference in the realm of hidden assumptions, and would perhaps result in a history of a different texture from that of a man who was in every respect a materialist. If I chose to, I could write history with an eye on Providence and on *moral* progress, just as Marx and Carr have written with their eyes on social progress. But, I repeat, I don't think the City of God need come into our story about the Worldly City. Perhaps we can't write about the City of God at all; we don't have any historical evidence for it. I know all this sounds very priggish; it's not fashionable to say this sort of thing nowadays."

A bell, thin and light, like the upper register of a church peal, tinkled somewhere, and Butterfield stood up. "That means lunch is on the table," he said. Walking downstairs, he told me that while he and Carr were on the best of terms — in Oxford historians were foes, I gathered, and in Cambridge they were friends — the two of them had been carrying on a lively correspondence about matters they disagreed on. In the dining room, which was oak-panelled, like the study, Butterfield seated himself at a corner of the big table and talked some more about his disagreements with Carr. "Carr," he said, eating some melon, "is too much interested in society, to the exclusion of individuals. For instance, he says that if you cannot find out whether Richard III killed the princes in the Tower — the evidence is confusing — then you must find out if other kings killed princes in towers at that period. If they did, we can take it for granted that Richard III did the same. So what, I have to ask, if other kings killed princes? Our interest ought to be in Richard III. It's not only that as a Christian my interest is in the the individual, but . . ."

The maid, who was as formal as Butterfield was informal, served roast lamb, roast potatoes, and cauliflower, but Butterfield's talk could not be arrested by food. As I soon found out, he had set off on a scholastic argument with Carr, and not even his maid could rein him in. In a moment, he had left the table, rushed upstairs, and returned with Carr's book "What Is History?," which he handled less as if it were a Bible than as if it were a script of heretical writing. "In 1931," he said, leafing through the pages while his roast lamb, roast potatoes, and cauliflower got colder and colder, "I published my third book. In it I took to task a historical orthodoxy — the Whig interpretation of history, which had blighted the true study of English history for more than a hundred years. For the Whig historians — our nineteenth-century fathers — the whole of English history, from the Magna Carta to the constitutional gains of the nineteenth century, was simply one long battle between the forces of light and the forces of darkness, between the forces of liberty and the forces of despotism. Here is Carr's gloss to the book."

Having taken some sips of ginger ale, Butterfield mounted the altar of disputation. " 'In the iconoclastic 1930's . . .' " he began, reading aloud from his text with boyish exuberance, and obviously relishing the contretemps of the lunch; his voice resounded with quiet confidence, not the confidence of the righteous but that of the man who has possession of his audience.

". . . when the Liberal Party had just been snuffed out as an effective force in British politics [he read on], Professor Butterfield wrote a book called 'The Whig Interpretation of History,' which enjoyed a great and deserved success . . . not least because, though it denounced the Whig interpretation over some 130 pages, it did not . . . name a single Whig except Fox, who was no historian, or a single historian save Acton, who was no Whig. . . . The reader was left in no doubt that the Whig interpretation was a bad thing, and one of the charges brought against it was that it . . ."

As Butterfield came now to his own words in the little book, he quickened the tempo of his reading:

" '. . . studies the past with reference to the present' [the constitutional battle of the nineteenth century]. On this point, Professor Butterfield was categorical and severe. 'The study of the past with one eye, so to speak, upon the present, is the source of all sins and sophistries in history. . . . It is the essence of what we mean by the word "unhistorical.". . . ' "

His voice returned to its normal pace:

"Twelve years elapsed. The fashion for iconoclasm went out. Professor Butterfield's country was engaged in war often said to be fought in defence of the constitutional liberties embodied in the Whig tradition, under a great leader who constantly invoked the past 'with one eye, so to speak, upon the present.' In a small book called 'The Englishman and His History,' published in 1944, Professor Butterfield not only decided that the Whig interpretation of history is the 'English' interpretation, but spoke enthusiastically of 'the Englishman's alliance with his history' and of the 'marriage between the present and the past.' To draw attention to these reversals of outlook is not an unfriendly criticism. It is not my purpose to refute the proto-Butterfield with the deutero-Butterfield, or to confront Professor Butterfield drunk with Professor Butterfield sober. I am fully aware that, if anyone took the trouble to peruse some of the things I wrote before, during, and after the war, he would have no difficulty at all in convicting me of contradictions and inconsistencies at least as glaring as any I have detected in others. Indeed, I am not sure that I should envy any historian who could honestly claim to have lived through the earth-shaking events of the past fifty years without some radical modifications of his outlook. My purpose is merely to show how closely the work of the historian mirrors the society in which he works. It is not merely the events that are in flux. The historian himself is in flux. When you take up a historical work, it is not enough to look for the author's name in the title-page: look also for the date of publication or writing — it is sometimes even more revealing."

"So, Carr's gloss to my text is that he and I and all other historians are products of our times and our societies," Butterfield said. He dropped the book beside his plate and picked up his knife and fork for the first time. "The *int*eresting thing," he continued, cutting his meat, "is that the passage in 'The Englishman and His History' to which Carr refers, while published in 1944, was written and delivered in a lecture, in 1938." He paused significantly. "It happens that I am living and can contradict a small part of Carr's sociological history. But what if I weren't? Indeed, even though I am alive, Carr refuses to take me at my word. When I wrote to him that the passage in question was composed in 1938, he immediately wrote back that he would like to look at that lecture. Don't you see, in his letter he handed me an implied threat: that I must have changed — perhaps just by a few words — the book from the lecture. Unfortunately for me, I don't happen to have a copy of the original lecture, so even though I am an alive fact, I am unable to budge Carr." He laughed heartily.

With the sweet, Butterfield lightly remarked that the reason he liked Toynbee was that, unlike most great historians, he was not as a person "a heavy." He said that while he agreed with Toynbee's method — "making generalizations of a higher and higher order, of course empirically, from the known facts" — he felt that Toynbee's generalizations, like Carr's theories, outran the facts.

Upstairs, over coffee, Butterfield talked a little bit about himself. "At school — in the West Riding of Yorkshire — I wanted to do classics," he said. "I don't think one can be a first-rate humanist without classics. But my headmaster wanted me to go into the scientific stream, because we didn't have Greek at the school. One day, he came to me and said, 'Butterfield, let's compromise on history.' I did. I read history there and at Peterhouse and have been working at it here one way or another for the past thirty years. I think I would have been a better historian with classics."

I didn't agree, and argued with him, but, like most English intellectuals, he had been bitten as a child by the classical bug — they separate the universe automatically into classics and science — and most of my points were vigorously, though kindly and charmingly, brushed aside. Afterward, the Master went on to talk a little about his intellectual preoccupations. "I don't believe in committee history, à la Namier — I believe in one-outlook history," he said. "Since 1939, I have been working intermittently on "The Cambridge Shorter Modern History' of Europe. I hope my 'History' will display some of the analytical gifts of Namier and some of the flow of Miss Wedgwood, but, unlike the Namierites, I don't mind if it is superseded one day by future research; I only hope it won't be superseded before I have finished writing it — like the works of inferior narrative historians. The life of Charles James Fox, the eighteenth-century statesman, is even closer to my heart than the European history. You know how it came about?"

I shook my head.

"Somebody told Trevelyan — he had a lot of the Fox papers in his possession — that my schoolboy ambition had been to write a biography of Fox. Just around that time, I had published my 'Whig Interpretation of History,' and Trevelyan, who was the last of the Whig historians, was rather put out with me. He felt sure that my book was a surreptitious attack on him personally. This was not true. Despite his hurt feelings, in 1930 he sent me the Fox papers, with his blessing. I was overwhelmed. I had actually hoped that Trevelyan himself would write the biography; in any case, I didn't truly feel that I had the mental equipment for Fox. Off and on since 1930, I've been working at the biography, but I have been so intimidated by my task that I have been bringing out monographs and little books on certain aspects of his life (his foreign policy, and the like) — books that, in the true tradition of the Namierites, sometimes covered no more than a year of Fox's activities. Someday, when I have published enough of these piecemeal studies, I shall perhaps be able to realize my schoolboy ambition. What has held me to Fox all these many years is his overpowering charm. The strange thing is that while everybody testifies to his charm, there is no evidence for it in the way he conducted himself. I mean, you look at his portrait and he appears fat and vulgar. You listen to the talk of his contemporaries and you discover he was quite a rogue. The papers of the period are full of his hurting people, his wrong deeds. But within six months all his deeds, all his wickedness were always forgiven. And everybody says that what did it was his charm. I am completely under his spell — the spell of his charm."

During my rounds, many historians had mentioned Lady Namier with affection and awe, and had praised her marriage with Namier. "For both, it was a second and a late marriage," one had said. "Both had been rather unhappy until they met each other; bad experiences in Eastern Europe, the homeland of both of them, had dogged them much of their lives. But their marriage turned out to be one of the happiest among historians in memory. I have never seen two people have such an impact on each other."

I now found Lady Namier, who lived in the Grampians, a block of flats near Shepherd's Bush, in Namier's study. It was a small room with white walls, blue hangings, a blue carpet, and — most prominent of all the furnishings — a dark-orange chair, which, I learned, had been his favorite chair at home. Lady Namier was a dignified woman, her face etched with deep lines of suffering. She was dressed in mourning, although more than a year had gone by since her husband's death. She showed me a sheltered balcony off the study, explaining that her husband used to spend his Sunday afternoons there when they didn't go out, and saying that she had lived at the Grampians with a woman friend for some years before her marriage to Namier, in 1947. They had often thought of getting a more spacious place, but once he had settled there he didn't want his books and papers moved, so they had stayed on year after year. We returned to the study, and she asked me to take the dark-orange chair.

"Because of my back, I prefer to sit in this," she explained, choosing a straight one. "I picked up my infirmities in Russia — in a concentration camp and in solitary confinement in prison — during the Stalin regime." I knew that she was a Russian by birth, and that her first husband had been Russian. Without any prompting from me, she went on, "At the beginning of the purges, my first husband and I had a rather disturbed career, you understand. For unknown reasons, we were sent into a sort of prison-exile in Central Asia — which meant Samarkand, and later Tashkent. In these camps, hunger was so bad — this was around 1930 — that there was cannibalism. When we arrived at the first of these places, there was a loud affair — in the papers and all that sort of thing — that patties with human meat in them were being served. Now, man doesn't eat man unless he must. Later, we were arrested on the charge that my husband was a terrorist and wanted to kill Stalin — whom, by the way, he had never seen — and that I knew all about his plot and the men who were implicated with him. I don't know what happened to him; he disappeared. I was put into solitary confinement in Moscow, where I became very ill. There was little to eat and nowhere to walk, my muscles went weak, my back broke, my hands and feet became frostbitten, and recently I've discovered that even the inside of my face was frostbitten, leaving me with a permanent sinus condition. When I was too sick to walk, I was pushed out, to lug myself and my sticks — my few belongings — about. I left Russia." Lady Namier said that under her maiden name, Iulia de Beausobre, she had written a book about her experiences, "The Woman Who Could Not Die." She explained that, perhaps because she was a writer, or perhaps because she had learned something from her solitary confinement, she had only two touchstones for her life — truthfulness and complete candor. "I am writing my biography of Lewis with these touchstones," she said. "I know that he would have liked it so."

Lady Namier's way of talking was overwhelming; she

emphasized practically every word, and everything she said, no matter how matter-of-fact, had a deep emotional content. I came to realize that although her enunciation gave the impression of nervousness, she was simply speaking English with the exaggerated clarity of a foreigner. While we talked, we faced a photograph of Namier's head and shoulders. His face was more impressive than attractive; a bony forehead and protruding cheekbones made his face seem narrow and also gave the impression of strength. "This picture was taken in Israel one spring," Lady Namier said. "I am waiting for Lewis's head in wood, which is coming any day. Physiologically, the most interesting thing about him was the back of his head, which was round and protuberant, like a dome. I have already written three chapters of Lewis's biography, but so far I am only up to his early days in Eastern Europe. He was born just outside Warsaw — in a country house — and he later lived in many parts of Poland, including the Russian and Austrian sections. While growing up, he acquired, as a matter of course, besides his own Polish language, German and Ukrainian, and, from his Polish governess, English. But Polish was always the language he spoke most beautifully, and because it was so different from English, he never succeeded in speaking English well. His written English, however, which he was always scrubbing and polishing, was another matter. After all, the century of his interest was a century of great English prose."

Lady Namier went into the kitchen and brought out a tray full of bananas, grapes, apples, and oranges. I took an apple, and she picked up a bunch of grapes. "Because of political troubles," she said, "the Namierowskis left Poland and settled for a time in Lausanne, Switzerland, where Lewis first heard the sociologist Vilfredo Pareto lecture. He followed him to the London School of Economics, where he was introduced one day to A. L. Smith, then Senior Tutor at Balliol, who immediately decided that Lewis belonged to Balliol. So at the age of twenty he found himself at the college." Having eaten two or three grapes, she said, "I live on fruits. Lewis was not a very sentimental man, but he was a deeply grateful one. He used to tell me that he always knew he had a good brain, a good mechanical apparatus, but that he really learned to use it at Balliol, at the feet of A. L. Smith. He said to me that the greatest honor of his life was to be made an honorary Fellow of the college. In 1930 or '31, he was given a chair at Manchester. In 1941 or '42, we met. The reason I am writing a biography of Lewis is that while many people understood him intellectually, no one understood his range of emotions. And his ideas would have been better understood if he had been able to write the fruit of his life's study, that survey of the English Parliament which John Brooke is writing now. But Lewis was a subtle, withdrawn man, and he would laugh even at his summaries of his own theories. Once, he said to Sir Isaiah Berlin — Isaiah was a little hurt; he thought Lewis was being unkind — 'You

must be a very clever man to understand what you write.'
About his interests — during his Galician childhood he
had injured his ears while hunting with an old gun, so
music meant nothing to him. He was worse than tone-
deaf. We did go and look at a lot of pictures, in Flor-
ence, in Siena, in Amsterdam, but whenever Lewis looked
at pictures, he thought only of his period, and what light,
if any, they threw on his history. Perhaps that's why
he preferred portraiture to any other form of painting.
A lot of people thought him a snob, because he was in
the company of lords and ladies, but he cultivated lords
and ladies mainly for their muniment rooms, which were
repositories of a wealth of historical documents. He had
no hobbies; he worked all the time. Naturally, we weren't
very social. But the tragedy of his life was that he never
slept. Oh, he did have one good night every few months,
and then he worked at his best the next day. It was by
comparison that the nights he didn't sleep seemed so
bad. He had to take pills to go to sleep, other pills to
wake up. He was therefore irritable. As I was saying,
the most interesting thing about him was the range of
his emotions. Though he was a Jew, he didn't basically
like Jews. Lewis believed in character, which he thought
was as fixed in all men as a stone in a ring; he didn't
like what had become of the Jewish character. He
thought that historical circumstances had made of the
Jew a *petit bourgeois* and a rootless creature; money had
taken the place of ties and roots. But Lewis, instead of
leaving the Jews there, became the most ardent Zionist

of his time, maintaining that the only way the Jews could become normal was to have roots, and the only place they could put down their roots was their original home, Palestine. His Zionism consisted of trying to join the land and the state."

I broke into the fast flow of her words to ask her the question that had brought me to her: "Did he apply to himself the same method of analysis that he applied to others? How did he go about analyzing, for instance, the source of his Zionism?"

"He did more than analyze himself," she said. "He was always being psychoanalyzed. First in Vienna in 1923 and '24, and then off and on in England for the rest of his life. He had this cramp — paralysis — in his right arm. It wasn't just a writer's cramp, and doctors told him that the cause was not physiological but psychological. That was the beginning of his psychoanalysis. In the twenties, his cramp wasn't so bad, but in the thirties, with the mounting mistreatment of Jews, his arm became almost useless. Indeed, Lewis was so terrified of the idea of a German occupation of England that he had one of his doctor friends give him a bottle of poison, which he always carried in his waistcoat pocket, so he could kill himself in case the Germans came. Not until the war was over could I make him throw the tablets away."

"What did psychoanalysis do for him?" I asked.

"It brought to the surface of his mind many, many things — such as the fact that his Zionism was really a result of the conflict between his Polish mother and his Galician father, and that his wish to unite the land and state of Israel was really an attempt to paper over childhood memories of his bickering parents. And his conservatism — he always insisted he was a radical Tory — he discovered was a result of his loneliness as a child and as a grownup. You see, he never hunted in a pack, he was always an outsider. Because he never learned how to *consort* with people, he wanted to find out the principles by which people consort with each other. And this is why he spent most of his life studying the politics of Parliament, and so on — because that was where people best consorted with each other. Not for nothing did he use an epigraph from Aeschylus' 'Prometheus Vinctus' for his 'Structure of Politics.'" Lady Namier went on to recite the lines: "'I took pains to determine the flight of crook-taloned birds, marking which were of the right by nature, and which of the left, and what were their ways of living, each after his kind, and the enmities and affections that were between them, and how they consorted together.' Again, he found that he was an imperialist because he thought the Romans had discovered the principle and had worked out a very good system of consorting together; they had preserved peace as a result of it. Like the Romans, the English had mastered the principle, and — individually, at least — were kind enough, humane enough, to teach it to their subjects, and Lewis thought that if their institutions were grafted onto other societies the

other societies would know how to consort also. He
spent his life studying group life — the very thing that
he didn't, he couldn't, have. But he by no means accepted Freud and psychoanalysis whole hog. He accepted the diagnostic half of Freud but not the thera-
peutic; he knew that his cramp was caused by the per-
secution of the Jews, yet his arm didn't get any better,
and he knew why he was a Zionist, yet he remained a
Zionist. His view of psychoanalysis, whether it was applied to the past or to him, was that it deepened one's
understanding without curing anything. The sex side
of Freud didn't engage him very much, either; he was
really never interested in the sexual lives of the M.P.s.
In that way, he was much more of a later Freudian,
for he believed the basic human impulse to be the death
wish. The death wish in Lewis himself was very strong,
and perhaps that is why he died so blissfully — very
blissfully. When I think of Lewis, I'm most thankful
that he had so little pain at his death. He was seventy-
two when he died. The day of his fatal illness, he rang
me up from the office to say not to prepare dinner at
home, as usual; he would pick something up en route,
so he could get to work that evening with a minimum
of interference. At that time, we were preparing a new
edition of that first volume of the 'American Revolution.'
He came home about six-thirty, and I heard fumbling
at the door. I knew immediately that it was Lewis, but
I also sensed that there was something wrong. I went
to the door and there he was, white as snow. He said

he'd been seized by the most violent pain, but, as usual, he'd come in the Tube — strap-hanging. I got him into bed, and called our doctor. He came, gave him an injection, said it was an inexplicable cramp, and assured me that when the pain wore off Lewis would be able to sleep — which he did. At four o'clock, however, Lewis knocked on the wall. I rushed in. He was in considerable distress. The telephone was at his bedside, and I didn't want to ring the doctor in front of him; I thought it would frighten him. Finally, I decided to do it, but he prevented me. 'The doctor was here late last night,' he said, 'and I don't want him disturbed at this terrible hour.' Then he looked up, radiant, and said, 'What a pity! Yesterday was the first time I saw in my mind's eye the survey of Parliament as a whole.' He died the next morning."

At home, reading over the notes on my various talks, I could, for one thing, hear the wits of Cambridge heckling Butterfield: "How can you judge Namier by the Namierites? Shouldn't you judge a school of thought by its best representative, Namier, rather than by its worst representatives, moles 'burrowing themselves into smaller and smaller holes'?" And "Isn't the point of education to make us skeptics — skeptics about ourselves and skeptics about others — rather than to beat us into receptacles for remote imaginary ideals and policies?" And "How can you in this day and age believe in the City of God? If God's history shouldn't exist, aren't you and Namier really saying the same thing — that human history in the last analysis is unknowable?" And, and, and . . .

If there were a rock of philosophy still standing, a Butterfield could hide behind it and avoid the tomatoes and onions of controversy. As someone has said, with a sleepy nod to his Greek predecessor, "I have read somewhere — in Dionysius of Halicarnassus, I think — that History is Philosophy teaching by examples." Even if the reverse should be the case — if philosophy should turn out to be incidental to history — still, without philosophy there could be no one acceptable history, no one way of doing it. But today, it seemed, there was no agreement, even on how to crack one of the oldest chestnuts in the philosophical fire, determinism. Were all thieves kleptomaniacs? Were the Genghis Khans and Adolf Hitlers helpless victims of circumstance? Should we therefore substitute the psychiatrist's couch for the hangman's noose?

Unless a philosopher finds for us an acceptable faith or synthesis — as Plato and Aristotle did together for their age, and St. Augustine, Thomas Aquinas, and Immanuel Kant for theirs — we remain becalmed on a painted ocean of controversy, and for better or worse, insofar as the past is a compass to the future, there will never be anyone to whistle thrice for us and say, once and for all, "The game is done! I've won! I've won!"

ABOUT THE AUTHOR

Ved Mehta is Indian by birth and American by naturalization. He was educated at Pomona College; at Balliol College, Oxford; and at Harvard. He has held two Guggenheim Fellowships and two extended Ford Foundation grants. In 1982, he was awarded a MacArthur Prize Fellowship. He has contributed articles and stories to many newspapers and magazines—primarily to *The New Yorker*. He has written books on Christianity (*The New Theologian*), on language (*John Is Easy to Please*), and on India and its leaders (*Walking the Indian Streets, Portrait of India, Mahatma Gandhi and His Apostles, The New India, and A Family Affair*). He is also the author of *Delinquent Chacha* (a novel), *Face to Face* (a youthful autobiography), *The Photographs of Chachaji* (an account of the production of an award-winning television film he helped create), *Mamaji* and *Daddyji* (biographies of his parents), and, most recently, *Vedi*.